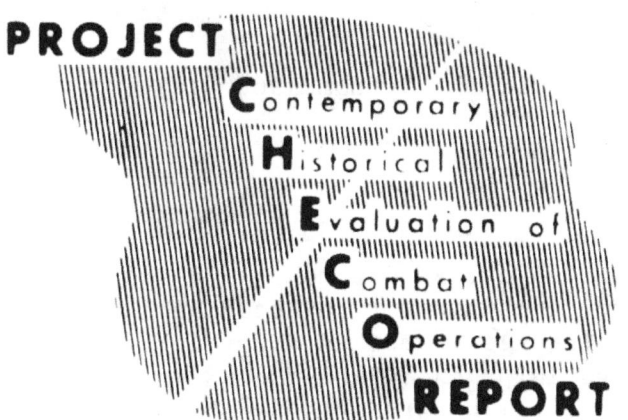

PROJECT CHECO REPORT
Contemporary
Historical
Evaluation of
Combat
Operations
REPORT

THE WAR IN VIETNAM
1966

23 OCTOBER 1967

HQ PACAF
Directorate, Tactical Evaluation
CHECO Division

Prepared by:
Mr. Wesley R. C. Melyan
Miss Lee Bonetti
SEAsia Team

REPLY TO
ATTN OF: DTEC 23 October 1967

SUBJECT: Project CHECO Report, "The War in Vietnam 1966" (U)

TO: SEE DISTRIBUTION PAGE

1. Attached is a TOP SECRET NOFORN document. It shall be transported, stored, safeguarded, and accounted for in accordance with applicable security directives. Each page is marked according to its contents. The information contained in pages marked NOFORN in this document will not be disclosed to foreign nationals or their representatives. Retain or destroy in accordance with AFR 205-1. Do not return.

2. Reproduction of this document in whole or in part is prohibited except with the permission of the office of origin.

3. This letter does not contain classified information and may be declassified if attachment is removed from it.

FOR THE COMMANDER IN CHIEF

EDWARD C. BURTENSHAW, Col, USAF
Chief, CHECO Division
Directorate, Tactical Evaluation

1 Atch
Proj CHECO SEA Rpt, (TSNF),
23 Oct 67

DISTRIBUTION

HQ USAF

AFAMA	1 Cy	(1)	AFSLP	1 Cy	(21)
AFCHO (Silver Spring)	2 Cys	(2,3)	AFSTP	1 Cy	(22)
AFFRA	1 Cy	(4)	AFXOP	1 Cy	(23)
AFGOA	2 Cys	(5,6)	AFXOPG	1 Cy	(24)
AFIGO	1 Cy	(7)	AFXOSL	1 Cy	(25)
AFIDI (Norton)	1 Cy	(8)	AFXOSN	1 Cy	(26)
AFISL	1 Cy	(9)	AFXOPR	1 Cy	(27)
AFNINDE	3 Cys	(10-12)	AFXOPH	1 Cy	(28)
AFNINCC	1 Cy	(13)	AFXOPFI	1 Cy	(29)
AFNINA	1 Cy	(14)	AFXOSS	1 Cy	(30)
AFOMO	1 Cy	(15)	AFXPD	9 Cys	(31-39)
AFPDP	1 Cy	(16)	AFXDOC	1 Cy	(40)
AFRDC	1 Cy	(17)	AFXDOD	1 Cy	(41)
AFRDR	1 Cy	(18)	AFXDOL	1 Cy	(42)
AFRDQ	1 Cy	(19)	SAFOI	2 Cys	(43,44)
AFSMS	1 Cy	(20)	SAFLL	1 Cy	(45)
			SAFAA	1 Cy	(46)

AIR UNIVERSITY

ASI-HA	2 Cys	(47,48)	AUL3T-66-7	1 Cy	(50)
ASI-ASAD	1 Cy	(49)	ACSC	1 Cy	(51)

MAJCOM

TAC (DPLPO)	2 Cys	(52,53)	SAC (DI)	1 Cy	(58)
MAC (MAFOI)	1 Cy	(54)	SAC (DXIH)	1 Cy	(59)
AFSC (SCL)	1 Cy	(55)	SAC (DPL)	1 Cy	(60)
AFLC (MCF)	1 Cy	(56)	USAFE (OPL)	2 Cys	(61,62)
ATC (ATXDC)	1 Cy	(57)	USAFSO (NDI)	1 Cy	(63)
			USAFSO (BIOH)	1 Cy	(64)

OTHERS

9AF (DO)	1 Cy	(65)	USAFTAWC (DA)	1 Cy	(69)
12AF (DAMR-C)	1 Cy	(66)	USAFTARC (DI)	1 Cy	(70)
19AF (DA-C)	1 Cy	(67)	USAFTALC (DA)	1 Cy	(71)
USAFSAWC (DO)	1 Cy	(68)	USAFTFWC (CRCD)	1 Cy	(72)
			FTD (TDFC) (W-P AFB)	1 Cy	(73)

PACAF

C	1 Cy	(74)	IG	1 Cy	(81)
DOP	1 Cy	(75)	DXIH	1 Cy	(82)
DP	1 Cy	(76)	5AF (DOP)	1 Cy	(83)
DI	1 Cy	(77)	13AF (DOP)	1 Cy	(84)
DO	1 Cy	(78)	7AF (CHECO)	9 Cys	(85-93)
DM	1 Cy	(79)	DTEC	3 Cys	(94-96)
DPL	1 Cy	(80)			

TABLE OF CONTENTS

	Page
FOREWORD	vii
PREFACE	viii

CHAPTER I - POLICIES AND STRATEGY 1

    Enemy Objectives and Strategy 1
    U.S. Objectives and Strategy 3
    CINCPAC's Three-Phase Strategy 7
    7AF OPLANS and OPORDS 8

CHAPTER II - RULES OF ENGAGEMENT AND RESTRICTIONS 9

    General Rules 9
    Authority 10
    Authorized Jettison Areas 11
    Rules of Engagement Definitions 12
    Demilitarized Zone Restrictions 14
    Cambodian/RVN Border Operations 16
    Laos Restrictions 17
    ROLLING THUNDER Restrictions 20
    Targets of JCS 22
    Recommended Changes to Rules of Engagement 23
    Border Violations 25
    Bombing Standdowns 31
    USAF Personnel Detainees 42

CHAPTER III - COMMAND AND CONTROL 44

    Centralized Air Control 44
    Airstrikes Review Board 47
    ARC LIGHT Program Control 50
    Route Package Assignments - North Vietnam 52
    ABCCC 53

CHAPTER IV - FRIENDLY AIR CAPABILITIES 55

    Mission 55
    Strength and Deployment 55
        SEA Deployments--April - December 1966 61
        Tactical Strike Squadrons in SEA by Month 62
    Vietnamese Air Force (VNAF) 66
    Base Construction 72
    MCP Funding Problems 73
    Project Turnkey 75

	Page
Tuy Hoa AB	75
Cam Ranh Bay AB	77
Phu Cat AB	77
Phan Rang AB	78
Base Defense	79
Logistics	83
Ordnance	83

CHAPTER V - FRIENDLY AIR OPERATIONS ... 90

- Introduction ... 90
- Interdiction - Aerial ... 90
- STEEL TIGER ... 91
- TIGER HOUND ... 92
- Operation TALLY HO ... 95
- ARC LIGHT Program ... 97
- ROLLING THUNDER ... 100
- North Vietnam Defenses ... 104
- Interdiction - Ground ... 108
    - Barrier System ... 108
- Area-Denial Weapons ... 113
- Primary Infiltration Routes ... 116
- Herbicide Operations ... 119
- Pink Rose ... 120
- Project Popeye ... 123
- Close Air Support and Direct Air Support ... 125
    - Introduction ... 125
- Major Ground Operations ... 127
    - Operation MASHER/WHITE WING ... 128
    - A Shau Special Forces Camp ... 128
    - Operation HAWTHORNE ... 130
    - Operation EL PASO ... 130
    - Operation ATTLEBORO ... 132
- ARC LIGHT ... 133
    - Reaction Time ... 136
    - Information Leaks ... 138
    - Tiny Tim ... 138
    - ARC LIGHT Assessment ... 138
- Reconnaissance ... 140
    - Out-of-Country Recce ... 142
    - Blue Springs ... 143
    - Project Phyllis Ann ... 144
- Airlift Operations ... 145
    - Organization ... 146
    - 2d Aerial Port Group ... 147
    - 315th Air Commando Wing ... 148
    - C-130 Force ... 149
    - Project Red Leaf ... 151
    - Emergency Airlift Request Systems (EARS) ... 153

	Page

    Psychological Warfare 154
    Search and Rescue 160

CHAPTER VI - CONCLUSIONS 165

    Assessment 165
    Rand Corporation Appraisal 173
    Summary of Results for 1966 175
    The Future 177
    Communist Chinese Intentions 180

FOOTNOTES

    Chapter I 182
    Chapter II 183
    Chapter III 188
    Chapter IV 190
    Chapter V 194
    Chapter VI 202

APPENDIX

    I - Attacks on Air Bases - 1966 204

FIGURES   Follows Page

    1. Air Bases in Thailand 18
    2. Sentry Dog and Handler in SEA 76
    3. Mortar Attack at Tan Son Nhut 82
    4. Xom Ca Trang Highway 90
    5. F-105 Thunderchief Pilots Destroy Bridge 100
    6. SAM Site Attacked with Fragmentary Rockets 104
    7. Gia Lam Airfield 106
    8. North Vietnamese MIG is Destroyed 108
    9. FAC Flies Daily Patrol 126
   10. Aerial View - A Shau SFC 128
   11. Airlifting Artillery to Field Forces 146
   12. Pararescue Crew Member 160

FOREWORD

"The War in Vietnam - 1966" is a sequel to "The War in Vietnam - 1965." It summarizes and places in perspective, the Air Force mission in Southeast Asia (SEA). The strategy of airpower in this area of conflict, its offensive and defensive air and ground operations, and effectiveness of command and control are also discussed. Future publications of "The War in Vietnam" will cover semiannual periods.

The comprehensive program of the Air Force--the complexity of its varied roles in SEA--called for more detailed studies of air and ground operations. It is recommended, therefore, that other Contemporary Historical Evaluation of Combat Operations (CHECO) reports be read in conjunction with "The War in Vietnam - 1966."

The 1966 chronology of "Organization and Deployments," published by the Seventh Air Force, provides a perspective of Air Force activities in SEA. The Thirteenth Air Force history of "The U.S. Air Force Buildup in Thailand - 1966" and "The USMACV Command History - 1966" are other valuable sources of information.

PREFACE

"...In Southeast Asia today, airplane-mounted weapons constitute our basic firepower. That in itself is unprecedented. But beyond that, new functions for airpower have come into being that were scarcely dreamed of as short a time ago as the Korea War.

"In a battlefield 10,000 miles from our shores, the airplane has become our basic supply vehicle. In a tropical area without roads or railways, aircraft have taken over the functions of field artillery and troop transport. On a war front that consists of hundreds of tiny, shifting combat areas, aircraft have become the equivalent of the mobile armored reserve. In a war where the enemy travels lightly under jungle cover, always seeking the advantage of surprise, aircraft have become our reconnaissance cavalry. There is scarcely a piece of equipment used in classical land warfare--supply truck, tank, troop carrier, mobile artillery, ambulance--whose function has not been substantially assumed by airplanes and helicopters--aircraft of every size and vintage, some brand new, some first produced more than 30 years ago.

"The U.S. now has a lot of brave men fighting and dying on foot in the jungle. It takes nothing away from them to say that the only thing that permits a few hundred thousand Americans the hope of victory on the land mass of Asia, where, a decade ago, more than 600,000 French troops failed, is the all-out use of the airplane...."

--"The Air War in Vietnam,"
FLYING, December 1966

CHAPTER I

POLICIES AND STRATEGY

Enemy Objectives and Strategy

At the end of 1966, the Commander, U.S. Military Assistance Command, Vietnam (COMUSMACV) made the following assessment of communist objectives:[1]

> "...As I view the situation over the past year, I conclude that the enemy's objectives did not change during the course of the year. They were, and still are, to first, extend his control over the people in South Vietnam; second, disrupt the Government of Vietnam's effort to extend its control over the people of its country; three, destroy the will of the GVN, the people of South Vietnam, the allied troops, and the people of the allied countries to resist Communist insurgency and aggressions; and four, bolster his own will to pursue his objectives of unifying Vietnam by force as a Communist state...."

The communist objectives as expressed by Hanoi and as reiterated by the Chinese Communists (CHICOMS) and the Union of Soviet Socialist Republics (USSR) could be summed up as follows:[2]

- To compel the U.S. to stop its bombing of North Vietnam;

- Cessation of U.S. "aggression";

- Adherence to the military provisions of the Geneva Agreements;

- Withdrawal of U.S. and "satellite" troops from South Vietnam;

- Settlement of internal affairs of the RVN by the South Vietnamese themselves, in accordance with the National Liberation Front (NLF), the political arm of the Viet Cong;

- U.S. engagement in negotiations with the NLF;

- Reunification by the Vietnamese themselves without foreign interference, and U.S. acceptance of North Vietnam's four-point stand, which called for the eventual reunification of Vietnam, and a political settlement in RVN in accordance with the Viet Cong program for a coalition government.

To achieve these objectives, the communists made it clear that they were willing to change the whole complexion of the fighting through enlargement of the war and destruction of the free Republic of South Vietnam. 3/

During 1966, the main strategy of the enemy appeared to be the isolation of Saigon and seizing of the highlands. He had created two, or possibly three divisions, and a special regiment to surround Saigon, dominate all routes leading into the city, isolate it economically, and create an atmosphere of physical insecurity. The enemy also had issued orders to dominate the highlands, and thus secure the terminus of his infiltration routes, and place sizable forces in the gateway to the coastal areas and to the south. The enemy's disposition of a division in Quang Ngai, one in Binh Dinh, and one in Phu Yen indicated his intent to retain control over large population centers, lines of communication, and to have access to rice, fish, and salt in the central coastal plains. This would also place him in a position to isolate U.S. spoiling attacks against his repeated attempts to carry out his plans. The political upheaval in I CTZ undoubtedly influenced him to commit major forces throughout the DMZ before arrival of the northeast (NE) monsoon. His purpose could have been to pull friendly strength from other areas, to create casualties, and most probably to seize as much terrain as possible south of the DMZ for psychological and political purposes. 4/

The enemy tactic of thorough, deliberate reconnaissance, early registration of weapons, detailed rehearsals, and prior preparation of the battlefield had given the U.S. forces time to detect his plans and launch spoiling attacks during 1966. Furthermore, his base areas were no longer secret or safe. Consequently, he was using, to an increasing extent, Cambodia, Laos, and the DMZ as sanctuaries during the year. 5/

The enemy continued to emphasize mobile warfare. All indications were that he intended to continue his protracted war of attrition into 1967. There was no evidence indicating that the enemy main forces intended to revert to Phase I or guerrilla-type operations. 6/

U.S. Objectives and Strategy

The pronouncements by the enemy and the failure of Hanoi to respond to the U.S. peace offensives during 1966, indicated a long and grinding process of hunting down the Viet Cong and NVN infiltrators and of pacifying Viet Cong-held villages and areas one by one. It was believed early in 1966, that more U.S. deployments of troops and aircraft, more airstrikes into the north and along the infiltration routes and staging areas of supplies going south, would be required. This would mean greater intensity of search-and-destroy operations, greater use of close air support, and augmented exploitation of aerial psychological warfare and special operations such as aerial defoliation of enemy operating-and-hiding areas. 7/

To counter the enemy's strategy to sustain military pressure in South Vietnam by his war-making capacity and his ability to infiltrate men and materiel into the south, the Secretary of Defense, Robert S. McNamara, in late 1965 wanted a guideline for planning military operations in SEA. Accordingly, early in December, he assigned to JCS and other interested parties, the requirement to coordinate a conference at Honolulu to work out this guideline. 8/

The Honolulu Conference had on its agenda the preparation of a wrap-up of a capabilities program for the continuation of the military operations in SEA in 1966. It also considered deployments of additional US/Free World Military Assistance Forces (FWMAF) in SEA. Deployment of additional personnel and materiel to the Pacific Command also was considered. The capabilities program included force lists, summary of forces, logistic matters, and deployment priorities on a monthly basis. Logistics included materiel tonnages, personnel replacement requirements, construction programs, transportation concept, and movement requirements. Determination of aircraft phasing included consideration of airfield availability, airfield construction, and completion dates. 9/

The conference identified four objectives, as well as strategy and tasks of air operations in SEA for 1966. The first objective of airpower was to make it as difficult and as costly as possible for the NVN to continue effective support of the Viet Cong, and to cause the government of NVN to cease directing the Viet Cong insurgency. The second objective for the use of air was to help in extending GVN domination, direction, and control over SVN. The third objective was to help defeat the Viet Cong and NVN forces in South Vietnam, and to force the withdrawal of NVN from the South. The last objective was to deter the Chinese Communists from direct intervention in SEA and to defeat them, should they choose to enter the conflict. [10]

To achieve these four objectives, the conferees determined that military strategy for employment of airpower would pursue five major aims: (1) the destruction of major enemy base areas in South Vietnam; (2) assistance in the liberation of selected areas which were being dominated by the Viet Cong; (3) selective destruction of the North Vietnamese war-supporting and war-making capability, and the wide-spread destruction, disruption, harassment, and attrition of the military and their support facilities, operations, and movements; and (4) assistance in defeating the Viet Cong and the North Vietnamese forces in South Vietnam. The final aim (5) was to help force the withdrawal of North Vietnamese forces from South Vietnam. [11]

The major tasks required to achieve the four basic objectives of airpower in SEA were presented in detail during the Honolulu Conference. To successfully realize the first objective, the following four tasks were provided: [12]

* Destroy the North Vietnam war-supporting and war-making capability by air attacks against enemy ports, power plants, communications facilities, POL and military installations, including the destruction of airstrike and air defense capability.

* Conduct border surveillance, cross-border, and counter-infiltration operations.

* Conduct air operations against PL/VM/PAVN Headquarters, communications facilities, supply lines and bases in Laos.

* Conduct air reconnaissance of infiltration routes through Laos and Cambodia into South Vietnam.

Six tasks were considered necessary to accomplish the second objective of extending GVN domination, direction, and control over South Vietnam: 13/

* Assist the RVNAF to defend major political, economic, food-producing and population centers, and strengthen the RVNAF offensive capability.

* Assist the RVNAF in clearing, securing, and civic action operations.

* Assist other U.S. agencies in their efforts to support the GVN in the development of those areas which have the greatest population or food-producing capability.

* Help enlarge, expand, connect, and consolidate secure areas in SVN.

* Assist and reinforce other U.S. Mission agencies, FWMAF, and the GVN in providing relief, reorientation, rehabilitation, and resettlement of refugees.

* Help reopen and maintain lines of communication in South Vietnam.

To attain the third objective to defeat the Viet Cong and NVN forces in RVN and to force the withdrawal of the NVN forces, seven tasks were envisioned: 14/

* Mount sustained, coordinated offensive operations against the enemy.

* Conduct a continuous harassing and destructive air offensive against major enemy war zones.

* Conduct raids and special operations against high priority targets in enemy war zones and base areas.

* Render major Viet Cong war zones unusable and destroy food stocks and war supplies in these base areas.

* Isolate enemy units from major political, economic, food-producing and population areas.

* Force the Viet Cong into sparsely populated food-short areas.

* Provide airlift and close air support to ARVN, Regional Popular and FWMA forces.

Six tasks were envisioned to attain the objective of deterring the CHICOMS from direct intervention in SEA and to defeat them if they should enter into the conflict: 15/

* Continue to improve operating and logistic air bases in the Western Pacific.

* Maintain forward deployments of air forces in the Western Pacific and be prepared to commit other forces in event of contingencies.

* Advise, support, and strengthen the Thai armed forces.

* Build, operate, and maintain selected bases, ports, airfields, communications centers, and logistical installations, and improve LOCs in Thailand.

* Plan and prepare to assist in counterinsurgency operations in Thailand, initially in the northeast, to restrict external support of subversion from Laos.

* Be prepared to employ nuclear weapons to destroy enemy military targets in South China and North and South Vietnam, should deterrence fail and the CHICOMS overtly intervene with combatant air, ground, or naval forces.

CINCPAC's Three-Phase Strategy

On 5 September, the Commander in Chief, Pacific (CINCPAC), presented his military strategy for the attainment of U.S. objectives in SEA. The strategy entailed a concept of integrated operations against Laos, North Vietnam, and the enemy in-country. The key to the strategy was that action in these three areas would be considered as interdependent undertakings. Selective applications of air and naval potential would hit the war-making and war-supporting capacities in the north. The logistic and personnel movement along the LOCs in Laos would be interdicted with aggressive relentlessness. The enemy and his infrastructure would be sought out and destroyed in the South. 16/

7AF OPLANS and OPORDS

There were thirty-three 7AF Operations Plans and Operations Orders active at the end of 1966. 17/

CHAPTER II

RULES OF ENGAGEMENT AND RESTRICTIONS

General Rules

The general Rules of Engagement for operations in SEA as of September 1966, authorized the U.S. forces in that area to attack and destroy any hostile aircraft or vessel. They could also assault hostile ground forces which attacked U.S. or friendly forces in RVN. The rules provided that in the event U.S. forces were attacked by hostile forces in RVN, Thailand, NVN, Cambodia, or SEA international waters or airspace, U.S. forces could conduct immediate pursuit over international waters or into territorial seas or airspace of Laos, Cambodia, or NVN when actually engaged in combat.[1]

If U.S. forces were attacked by hostile forces in Laos, according to the general rules, they could conduct immediate pursuit over SEA international seas or airspace of RVN and Thailand. Immediate pursuit of hostile aircraft originating in Laotian airspace, however, was authorized into NVN or Cambodian airspace only when actually engaged in combat.[2]

Under the limitations of these rules, when U.S. forces entered unfriendly territorial land, sea, or airspace in immediate pursuit, they were not authorized to assault other unfriendly forces or installations encountered unless attacked by them first. Even in this instance, the counterattack could be made only to the extent necessary for self-defense.[3]

The general rule stated that to declare an aircraft or vessel as hostile had to be tempered with judgment and discretion. It was pointed out that cases could occur where the destruction of Communist Bloc forces would be contrary to U.S. and allied interests. Examples were given of communist civilian aircraft discovered over RVN, Thailand, or Laos, which were off-course due to navigational errors and communist crafts trying to surrender. It was extremely important that full assessment be made of the pertinent factors and all available information and intelligence in determining actions to be taken. 4/

There was nothing in the rules that modified the requirement of a military commander to defend his unit against armed attack with all the means at his disposal. Another underlying guideline was that the commander concerned, in the event of such an attack, would take immediate aggressive action against the attacking force. 5/

Authority

The authority to declare aircraft hostile which were outside of friendly territory, but whose course, speed, and altitude posed a threat to friendly territory, based on intelligence information or circumstantial evidence, would be retained by the Commander, Mainland Southeast Asia Air Defense Region (Commander, 7AF), or his designated representative. 6/

Authority to engage an aircraft that had been visually identified as a Communist Bloc aircraft over-flying RVN-Thailand territory without proper clearance, or designated as a hostile aircraft by the U.S. Director of a Tactical Air Control Center (TACC) or his authorized representative, was

10

retained by the Commander, 7AF, or his authorized representative. 7/

Authorized Jettison Areas

The rules provided that in case of serious emergencies, aircrews could jettison ordnance "safe" in any uninhabited area in RVN, Thailand, Laos, or NVN. For the ROLLING THUNDER area, external stores could be jettisoned at the discretion of the aircrew or flight leader concerned, under emergency conditions, or if attack by enemy aircraft was imminent. For the BARREL ROLL (BR)/STEEL TIGER (SL) area, there was no free zone for jettison of live ordnance in Laos. In emergencies, ordnance (except napalm) could be dropped armed, under visual conditions, on any motorable trail, road, ford, or bridge within the BR/SL Armed Recce areas. Including napalm, it could be jettisoned armed under visual or under ground radar control in specifically designated areas contained in 7AF OPORD 433-67. Ordnance would not, however, be jettisoned in villages. 8/

The 7AF Commander, on 7 September, issued a compilation of the Rules of Engagement which applied at that time to the conduct of tactical operations in Southeast Asia. These rules consolidated various directives issued by JCS, CINCPAC, and MACV. For example, specific rules of ROLLING THUNDER operations were contained in 7AF OPORD 100-67; those for BARREL ROLL/STEEL TIGER operations were contained in 7AF OPORD 433-67. The 7AF Commander noted that the various Rules of Engagement, along with published changes to them, were directives--compliance was mandatory. He observed that violations could cause serious international repercussion and embarrassment to the United States. 9/

To insure that all units of 7AF and those under its operational control were familiar with every provision of the existing Rules of Engagement, PACAF Regulation 55-20 directed that a quarterly examination be given to each tactical aircrew member, interceptor pilot, weapons controller, and all personnel in the command and control structure. 10/

The 7AF Commander stated that tactical units would emphasize the responsibility of aircrews in regard to the Rules of Engagement, the buffer zones, borders, and restricted areas. He instructed that each pilot be intimately familiar with the CHICOM border, the immediate pursuit zone, and the restricted areas. The aircrews would make note of all circumstances concerning the Rules of Engagement and border warnings, or violation incidents which involved their flight. He further instructed that any aircrew member noticing another aircraft inadvertently proceeding toward a dangerous proximity of the CHICOM border, or other restricted areas, would take positive action to warn and divert such an aircraft. 11

Rules of Engagement Definitions

The 7AF Commander, in September 1966, provided the following definitions: 12/

SEA

SEA included the airspace, land mass, and territorial/internal waters of: (1) Thailand, Laos, Cambodia, North and South Vietnam; (2) the international waters and airspace of the Gulfs of Siam and Tonkin, and of the South China Sea in or over which U.S. forces operated in relation to U.S. objectives in SEA.

12

TERRITORIAL SEAS

This was a belt of sea adjacent to the coastal state three miles in breadth measured from the low water mark along the coast. However, in the states claiming over three-mile territorial seas, that distance would be observed for these rules as if it were the width of their territorial seas: (1) Thailand--six miles presumed; (2) Cambodia--five miles; (3) South Vietnam--three miles presumed; (4) North Vietnam--12 miles presumed; (5) Communist China--12 miles. Internal waters were waters to landward of the territorial seas.

TERRITORIAL AIRSPACE

This was defined as the airspace above the land territory, internal waters, and territorial seas of a sovereign country.

IMMEDIATE PURSUIT

This was defined as pursuit initiated in response to actions or attacks by hostile aircraft or vessels as defined in the Rules of Engagement. The pursuit had to be continuous and uninterrupted and could be extended as necessary and feasible over territorial/international airspace/seas as prescribed in the rules.

FRIENDLY FORCES

Friendly forces included all South Vietnamese (RVN), Royal Thai (RTG) and Royal Laotian (RLG) air, ground, and naval units and all other non-U.S. air, ground, and naval units operating with the RVN, RTG, RLG, and included such quasi-official organizations as Air America and Continental Air Service.

HOSTILE AIRCRAFT (SEA Except Cambodia and Laos)

A hostile aircraft was defined as one which was visually identified or was designated by the U.S. Director of a TACC, or his authorized U.S. representatives, as a Communist Bloc aircraft operating in RVN-Thailand territorial airspace without proper clearance from the government concerned; or observed in one of the following acts: (1) Attacking or acting in a manner which indicated with reasonable certainty an intent to attack U.S./friendly forces or installations; (2) Laying mines without permission of the government concerned within friendly territorial seas or internal waters; (3) Obviously not in distress, releasing free drops, parachutes, or gliders over friendly sovereign territory without permission of the government concerned. This included the unauthorized landing of troops or material on friendly territory.

HOSTILE AIRCRAFT--LAOS

As agreed by the RLG, a hostile aircraft in Laos was one visually identified, or was designated by the U.S. Director of a TACC, or his authorized U.S. representatives, as a Communist Bloc or Cambodian aircraft operating in Laotian territorial airspace observed in acts cited previously.

Any hostile aircraft needed to be identified visually only when a possibility existed that the aircraft was either friendly or non-military; i.e., civilian carriers or ICC aircraft.

HOSTILE VESSEL

A hostile vessel was defined as a surface or subsurface craft in RVN or Thailand internal waters and territorial seas, or SEA international waters, engaged in one of the following acts: (1) Attacking or acting in a manner which indicated within reasonable certainty an intent to attack U.S./friendly forces or installations, including the unauthorized landing of troops or material on friendly territory; (2) Laying mines within friendly territorial seas or internal waters without permission of the government concerned; (3) Engaged in direct support of attacks against RVN or Thailand; (4) When agreed to by RLG, a vessel in Laos internal waters which attacked U.S. friendly forces.

Demilitarized Zone Restrictions

Operations in the Demilitarized Zone (DMZ) started in July 1966, and on 13 July, CINCPAC was approached to provide the Rules of Engagement for operations in that area. COMUSMACV informed CINCPAC that pending receipt of these rules, friendly forces conducting operations in the immediate vicinity of the DMZ would take necessary action or counteractions against VC/NVA forces. He said this might involve returning of fire or maneuvering into the DMZ, for the purpose of attaining objectives in RVN or in exercising the right of self-defense. [13/] On 18 July, CINCPAC brought this to the attention of JCS, stating: [14/]

> "...Recommend we decide now, as a matter of urgency, to permit air operations and artillery fire from SVN against identified military activity within the DMZ. If concentrations of enemy troops develop in the DMZ, we should be prepared to consider authorization for friendly ground forces to conduct operations in that portion of the DMZ south of the Ben Hai River. There are adequate legal precedents relating both to the Korean Armistice Agreement and the Geneva Accords of Vietnam for operations on our part, which would be unlawful under the agreement, but which we have taken and justified because of similar conduct in violation of the agreements by the enemy. Our freedom of action should not be restricted beyond what the enemy is himself doing."

Shortly after obtaining JCS and State Department approval, CINCPAC granted COMUSMACV authority on 26 July, to conduct airstrikes in the DMZ. Civilian casualties would be minimized and no public disclosure would be made of the DMZ operations, except in accordance with instructions which were to be provided by Washington. [15/] In early August, all allied forces in RVN were instructed on the Rules of Engagement for the DMZ. [16/]

Early in September, according to the Rules of Engagement, strikes near the DMZ had to be against pre-briefed valid targets, which were clearly identified as being outside the DMZ. These targets were identified with certain procedures: (1) Flights conducting strikes within 50 nautical miles (NM) north of the DMZ would check in with Waterboy Control Reporting Point (CRP). Waterboy would make positive flight identification and would assist in placing the flight at the target coordinates. (Ground equipment limitations also had to be recognized.) Flights would use all available navigational equipment to positively identify their position. In this connection, the Tactical Air Control and Navigation (TACAN) channel 45 would be used for Distance Measuring Equipment (DME) and radial information. (2) Flights conducting strikes within 20 NM of the DMZ would have their position confirmed by Waterboy before attacking, or the flight had to be directed by a FAC. If a flight were merely in transit from south to north or north to south, the aircraft would detour either to the east or west, and would not approach any closer than five NM to the east or west of the DMZ.

Authority was granted to conduct airstrikes into the DMZ against clearly defined military activity identified and controlled by forward air controller (FAC) aircraft. The rules stressed that extreme care would be taken to prevent or minimize civilian casualties. The rule of thumb was: "When in doubt, do not attack." 17/

In December, COMUSMACV updated the Rules of Engagement for the DMZ, stating that they applied to US/FWMA forces only. Personnel in a position to influence RVNAF operations, conducted in or near the DMZ, however, would make every reasonable effort to insure that they were carried out under the Rules of Engagement as established for US/FWMA forces. 18/

Cambodian/RVN Border Operations

As of September 1966, the Rules of Engagement for planning operations near the Cambodian/RVN border stated that a request for approval for such action should be obtained in advance from COMUSMACV or his designated representative. This rule applied for initiated actions or counteractions against VC/PAVN forces, which might involve returning fire or maneuvering into Cambodia, either in attaining objectives in RVN or for self-defense.[19]

U.S. forces, in an emergency situation, were authorized to take necessary counteractions in the exercise of the right of self-defense against VC/PAVN attacks directed at US/allied forces from locations inside Cambodia. (In these instances, higher authority would be kept informed.) An emergency situation was considered to exist when, in the judgment of the commander, the urgency for taking timely counteractions in self-defense of US/allied forces precluded obtaining prior approval. Such counteractions could include airstrikes against enemy firing from the Cambodian side of the border against US/allied troops. No Cambodian forces would be engaged, except in self-defense; no Cambodian villages or populated areas would be attacked by air, artillery fire, or by ground forces. The intent of the rule provided for the defense of RVN, and the protection of US/RVN/FWMA forces. It specifically was not to be applied toward widening the conflict in Southeast Asia.[20]

In the last quarter of 1966, a policy was adopted whereby the Rules of Engagement for Cambodia would be republished or modified and updated quarterly. The second such republication was released by COMUSMACV on 23 December 1966.[21]

Laos Restrictions

In Laos, the RVN-based aircraft were cleared after the Christmas standdown in 1965, to support TIGER HOUND, YANKEE TEAM, and BARREL ROLL operations. Moreover, with JCS approval, authorization was given to conduct B-52 strikes against RLG authorized targets. In addition, Thai-based U.S. aircraft could be used for BARREL ROLL and STEEL TIGER for special close air support in specific areas. [22]/ Targets of opportunity could be attacked, day or night, if they were located within 200 yards of a motorable trail or road outside of a village. Fixed targets could be hit when they were RLAF priority-validated targets. Fixed targets or targets of opportunity could be struck, also, if AAA/AW were observed firing at friendly aircraft, or if these targets were approved by Vientiane or Savannakhet. [23]/

Special restrictions prohibited airstrikes near Laotian cities and friendly populated areas. Attacks could not be made within a radius of 25 NM of either Vientiane or Luang Prabang. Likewise strikes were prohibited within a radius of ten NM, or below an altitude of 15,000 feet, while attacking the enemy in the vicinity of Attopeu, Savannakhet, Thakhet, Saravano or Pakse. Restrictions also forbade strikes on campfires and civilian habitations.

Ordnance could not be expended in Xieng Khouang, Sam Neua, and Khang Khay. Unless permission was granted by the American Embassy in Vientiane, neither could it be dropped through overcast skies. [24]/ At the beginning of 1966, the Rules of Engagement authorized napalm (except in Laos), when it was considered absolutely essential in highly critical situations. [25]/

During a meeting held in January 1966 at Udorn, Thailand, COMUSMACV informed the Ambassador to Vientiane, that certain restrictions were

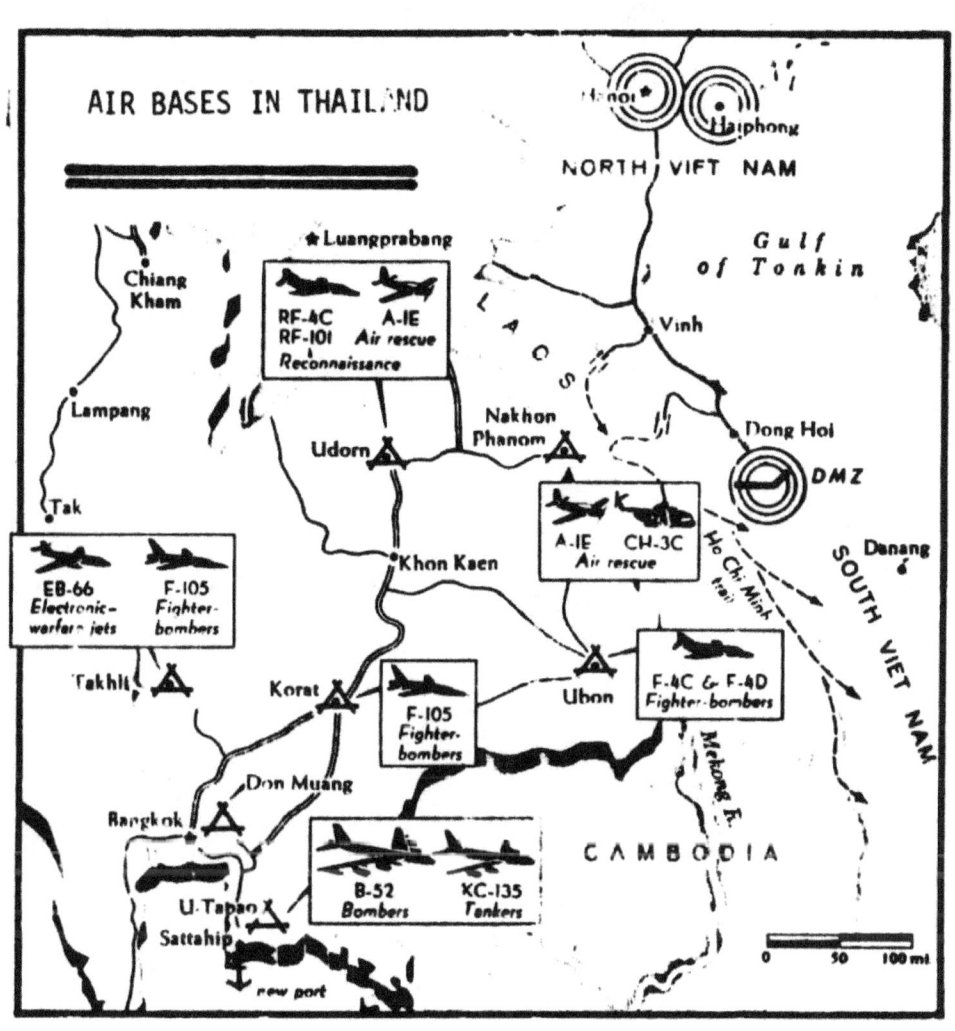

Figure 1

inhibiting attacks upon targets of opportunity, or targets escaping the TIGER HOUND area. The Ambassador's reactions were: [26]

1. It would be inadvisable to remove the restriction on the line of demarcation between TIGER HOUND and STEEL TIGER. He advised COMUSMACV, however, that he would reconsider his proposal after assuring the Laotians of the practicality of the TIGER HOUND system.

2. He granted permission for U.S. personnel to covertly install TACAN equipment in southern Laos. It complemented the existing sideband communications system in use between the RLAF at Savannakhet and Vientiane.

3. He interpreted the rules so that psychological warfare (psywar) leaflets might be dropped within the Laotian infiltration route areas.

4. Two RLAF observers were allowed access to the existing C-130 Airborne Command Post.

5. Greater use of napalm required the Secretary of State's decision. In late March 1966, the Secretary of State, citing the increased flexibility that napalm gave U.S. tactical air operations, extended the rules, so that use of napalm was permissible in the Laos Panhandle. Clearance subsequently was obtained by the American Ambassador in Vientiane from Premier Souvanna Phouma, for use of napalm in southern Laos, and, in principle, RLAF forces were also given the right to release it.

In the STEEL TIGER area, however, an additional restriction was imposed, as expenditure of napalm had to be confined to only RLAF-validated targets. Furthermore, expenditures required FAC control as defined in the Rules of Engagement for BARREL ROLL in southern Laos. No publicity as to the use of napalm in Laos was permitted, and all commanders and aircrew members were cautioned to prevent inadvertent strikes against villages, innocent inhabitants, and friendly troop positions. [27/]

In July, according to the Rules of Engagement, boats and barges on the Bang Fai River might be attacked between Mahaxay and Bun Nabok, if they were identified as military transports, and if such strikes were to be conducted under FAC control. Further extension of the rules permitted immediate pursuit of hostile aircraft into Laos. [28/]

ROLLING THUNDER Restrictions

Restrictions took many forms--in the Rules of Engagement for aircraft, in overflight control procedures, the use of napalm, and particularly in the selection of targets and areas to be struck. The 7AF Deputy Commander underscored some of these problems in August 1966 when he observed: [29/]

> "...Probably the most recognized and understood aspects of the 7AF operations in SEA are the conditions and limitations under which targets can be attacked. Not much more can be said on the subject which is not already known by all military personnel who are responsible for the conduct of the war. However, it is important to repeat for emphasis, the impact the limited air attack strategy has had on the effectiveness of Air Force operations and loss rates associated with our attacks.
>
> "In the main, 7th Air Force has been tasked to attack a relatively small number of targets many of which were of questionable value in a given space of time during the ROLLING THUNDER periods. This has forced us to channelize and stereotype our attack profiles and denied us the advantage of surprise and deception.
>
> "Due to the nature of the target and the defenses associated with them, sound tactics dictate the use of repeat attacks by

small numbers of aircraft. With limited targets available for airstrikes, we have been forced to make repeated attacks on the same targets until destroyed. Our pattern must be well known to the enemy. Once the first strike is made, he knows we will repeat until the target is destroyed. He can, therefore, take action to increase his defensive fire power against follow-on attacks. It is clearly in the interest of target destruction versus losses to allocate adequate lucrative targets sufficiently dispersed to permit the Air Commander to utilize the inherent capabilities of deception and surprise of the air weapons. This increased allocation of targets would not change the political limitations which are presently imposed but would permit greater freedom of action on those targets designated for attack."

Certain JCS' targets, such as dams and docks, were excluded from attack during 1966, while restrictions on others, such as POL targets, were gradually lifted during the year. The JCS-directed restriction had imposed an unprecedented control on the tactical operations of the 7th Air Force over North Vietnam.

At the beginning of the year, the program was restricted to the area south of Hanoi.[30/] On 1 April, the rules were relaxed by CINCPAC to allow strikes in the NE quadrant of North Vietnam, where the enemy had maintained a sanctuary.[31/] The rules were again relaxed in June, when authorization was given to attack all POL storage sites throughout North Vietnam, with the exception of those located within certain restricted zones. The restricted zones were defined as the area located within 30 NM of the center of Hanoi, ten NM from the center of Haiphong, or in the buffer zone, 25 NM from the CHICOM border east of $105°20'$ and 30 NM west of $105°20'$. This restriction was lifted after the Secretary of Defense and the Chairman of the Joint Chiefs of Staff had given their assurances that all means would be taken to minimize civilian casualties that might result from the strikes on the POL sites. [32]

Targets of JCS

The JCS' target list was originally conceived as a compilation of the most lucrative North Vietnamese targets, such as large, fixed installations of high military or economic significance. Because of overriding political considerations, the authorization to strike these targets was granted on a case-by-case basis by the Joint Chiefs, after consulting with higher authority and receiving their approval. Once clearance was obtained, the JCS targets were then generally available for restrike without additional clearance. Advance notice of the intent to restrike, however, was required for these targets. [33]

JCS' targets in North Vietnam totaled 242. Of this number, 168 or 69 percent had been struck at least once, since the bombing of North Vietnam started in August 1964. At the close of 1966, approximately 32 percent of the JCS' listed targets were not authorized for strike or restrike without prior JCS' approval. [34]

A comparison between the number of JCS' targets by Route Packages within North Vietnam, to the number of such targets that already had been struck reveals where the majority of targeting control was retained. In Route Package 6A (Air Force controlled), there were 58 targets, of which 32 had been struck. In Route Package 6B (Navy controlled), there were 54 targets, of which only 23 had been hit. Thus, only 49 percent of the targets in these two Route Packages had been struck and only 55 percent of the total designated targets were available for strike without prior JCS' approval. Within these two Route Packages, nearly half of the air space was "off limits," being classified as restricted or prohibited. This included the area within 30 NM of the Chinese border, all space within a radius of 30 NM of Hanoi, and that within 10 NM of Haiphong.

No strike flights were permitted in prohibited areas without specific JCS approval; furthermore, no targets of opportunity could be struck in the restricted areas. Hanoi alone contained 56 JCS' targets, of which 37 or 66 percent were not authorized for strikes without prior approval. Of the ten JCS' targets in the Haiphong area, six were not authorized for strike. Of the seven vital industrial sites in North Vietnam, only one was hit by the end of 1966. Of the six MIG-capable airfields in North Vietnam, none were authorized for attack in 1966. [35]

Recommended Changes to Rules of Engagement

CINCPAC was advised on 30 June 1966, that JCS had recommended to higher authority, a number of substantive changes which should be made to their basic Rules of Engagement pertaining to Southeast Asia. These recommendations along with responses of higher authority were:

1. U.S. forces should be allowed to conduct immediate pursuit of hostile aircraft into Communist China in response to attacks against them. [36] Higher authority responded:

> "...The current Rules of Engagements, as promulgated in JCS 009294/170122Z, April 1965, are clear and unequivocable regarding incursions into Communist China and

23

> reflect current U.S. Government policy: 'No pursuit is authorized into territorial seas or air space of Communist China.' In the event that Communist Chinese forces become directly involved in hostilities in Southeast Asia, this rule would obviously require reconsideration, and under such circumstances, I am confident that Chinese territory would not be accorded the status of a 'sanctuary'."

2. U.S. forces should be allowed to conduct immediate pursuit of hostile aircraft, ground forces, and vessels into Cambodia and Laos. Higher authority stated that existing special instructions regarding operations in the vicinity of the Cambodian border seemed adequate under existing circumstances. They added that existing special instructions were subject to further consideration on an urgent basis when situations warranted such action. 37/

3. U.S. forces should be allowed to conduct search-and-rescue (SAR) operations in Communist China when the risk of engagement would be small, or when there were clear prospects for a successful recovery. Higher authority replied: 38/

> "...As regards SAR operations, I am unaware of any restraints other than those dictated by good judgment and the capability of SAR forces and equipment, that would in any significant way reduce the effectiveness of these operations...."

Their response was qualified by this statement: 39/

> "...Nothing in these rules modifies in any manner the requirement of a military commander to defend his unit against armed attack with all means at his disposal. In the event of such attack, the commander concerned will take immediate aggressive action

against the attacking force...."

The JCS informed CINCPAC that their basic Rules of Engagement in Southeast Asia (JCS message 009294/170122Z Apr 65, modified by JCS message 002838/261447Z May 65), would remain in effect until they were advised differently. 40/

Border Violations

During 1966, the 7AF took action to avoid unauthorized overflights and border violations. In early April 1966, the 7AF observed that the greatest number of violators were U.S. Army and USAF aircraft. On 2 April, the 7AF Commander warned his subordinate commands that continued overflights of international borders could create an international incident, which might cause considerable embarrassment to the U.S. Government. He instructed that 7AF aircraft on in-country missions were not to cross international borders, unless they had specific authorization to do so. 41/

On 25 March 1966, in reply to CSAF's request for prescribed boundary data, 7AF advised him that no boundaries had been placed on missions since 24 December 1965, which required pilots to fly on a prescribed course to and from a designated NVN target area. Before each strike mission, CSAF was further advised, pilots were briefed at unit level on recommended approach and exit routes. These recommendations were based on known or suspected AAA and SAM sites, as well as concentrated automatic weapons positions.

The 7AF observed further that the strike mission commander could, in the majority of instances, determine the approach and exit route to and from the target area, based on such factors as changing weather conditions, sun position, ground fire encountered, etc. In NVN, area restrictions pertained to only those restricted areas which had been designated by the JCS. For South Vietnam and Laos, the only restrictions were those related to friendly areas. 42/

On 25 May, the 630th Combat Support Group's Tactical Unit Operations Center (TUOC) at Udorn, noted that Trojan Horse missions had been fragged to fly as close as four miles from the CHICOM border with fighter escort. Nearly all the missions penetrated the 30-mile buffer zone in NVN and these missions approached to within 10 miles of the CHICOM border in Laos. The Silver Dawn Orbit 5F4-531 had its northern turn-point at a distance of only 25 miles from the Laos-CHICOM border. Reference was made to four 7AF documents (7AF TS Commander 09121 May 66; 7AF OPORD 503-66; 7AF OPORD 100-66; and 7AF DOCO-P-L-TS 03878 Feb 66 OPS ORD 433-66), however, none of these contained guidance or restrictions concerning flying in the vicinity of the Burma-Laos or CHICOM-Laos borders. 43/

The 630th CSG, therefore, requested 7AF to provide immediate guidance and explicit Rules of Engagement to protect reconnaissance aircraft in these border areas. 44/

On 23 May, the 35th Tactical Fighter Wing (TFW), Da Nang Air Base, informed 7AF of their need for positive clarification of ECM cover procedures. This request was made because of the seriousness of an alleged Chinese border violation by the RB-66 and F-4 escorts, which occurred on 12 May.

Complying with this request, the 7AF issued these guidelines in May:[45]

> "There must be no doubt in the minds of the aircrews escorting other aircraft as to their primary mission: protection of the escorted aircraft. At least one element should remain in proximity of the aircraft being escorted. The distance out will be consistent with the effectiveness and the capability of the escort aircraft's radar and weapons system.
>
> "Every conceivable precaution in flight planning and conduct of the actual mission must be taken to prevent border violations. It must be absolutely clear that aircrews must not violate the rules under any circumstance."

After the Commander, 35th TFW, required refinement of these guidelines, 7AF on 25 June, clarified and expanded the Rules of Engagement for aircraft escorting reconnaissance vehicles:[46]

"Silver Dawn/Big Eye in the Gulf of Tonkin

The 7AF instructed that aircraft which had been fragged to escort any of these reconnaissance vehicles would remain with the aircraft being escorted. In addition, necessary cross checks would be carried out between the escort aircraft and the escorted aircraft for the purpose of authenticating the position of the aircraft. Such cross checks were mandatory as a measure to prevent a border or buffer violation. The 7AF added that, regardless of location, the escort aircraft was authorized to engage enemy aircraft which posed a threat to the escorted aircraft. However, the escort would advise if the reconnaissance aircraft was about to penetrate known restricted areas. The rule would be that, if contact could not be made, then the escort aircraft would stay with the escorted aircraft regardless of location. Moreover, the escort aircraft would attempt to divert the reconnaissance aircraft out of the restricted areas. The instructions promulgated that the escort aircraft would maneuver no closer than 30 nautical miles to the Communist Chinese border west of 106 degrees or 25 nautical miles east of 106 degrees while escorting any of the above listed reconnaissance aircraft outside of the restricted areas. Hot pursuit of enemy aircraft, however, was authorized to within 12 nautical miles of the Communist Chinese border."

"Silver Dawn in Laos

The 7AF instructed that the rules given above would apply with one exception. This exception was that the Silver Dawn escort aircraft were authorized specifically to escort the C-130 aircraft to the northernmost point of orbit 5F531. Moreover, the C-130 aircraft did not have to be advised of a penetration of a buffer zone unless the aircraft proceeded beyond that point."

"Trojan Horse

The same rules would apply as those above pertaining to the Gulf of Tonkin with one exception. This exception was that fighter aircraft, while escorting the U-2 aircraft, would maneuver no closer than 30 nautical miles from the Communist Chinese border. Moreover, surveillance of the U-2 aircraft would be maintained on radar when the flight was closer than 30 nautical miles to the Communist Chinese border. The 7AF instructed, however, that escort aircraft were allowed to attack without visual identification any aircraft that was approaching the Trojan Horse from the north or northeast above 36,000 feet and that was posing a threat to the U-2 aircraft. The 7AF instructed that hot pursuit could be continued up to 12 nautical miles from the Communist Chinese border when the enemy aircraft no longer posed a threat to the U-2 aircraft."

"Blue Springs

The 7AF instructed that aircraft escorting drones would escort only to the point identified in the fragmentation order. Moreover, such aircraft, in no case, would penetrate any of the restricted areas, nor would they go any closer than 30 nautical miles to the Communist Chinese border west of 106 degrees east, or 25 nautical miles east of 106 degrees east, or penetrate known SAM defended areas."

The 7AF, on 18 June, told Headquarters USAF and PACAF that they had changed border violation procedures on 2 June 1966, and established new warning instructions. Warning would be issued on the guard channel when friendly aircraft were within 30 NM of the Communist Chinese border, west of 106 degrees. Under this instruction, the China mainland and the Hainan Island shorelines would be considered as part of the Communist Chinese border. Warnings, as appropriate, would continue to be given through the buffer zone and in the Communist Chinese airspace. [47]

On 6 June, 7AF established the Panama Combat Reporting Center (CRC) as a single agency, which would be responsible for verification and documentation of border violation warning transmissions. Border violation warnings could be issued by Big Eye, Panama, AAW/SAR, DD, and other elements of TF77. The 7AF informed USAF and PACAF that bogus violation code words were being issued twice a week on a random time basis so as to exercise the system. They indicated on 18 June, that further recommendations on the warning system would be furnished after making a detailed on-the-site evaluation. They were also aware of emergencies and rescue activities involving use of guard channel, which took precedence over the warning data transmitted over the same frequency. [48]

As a result of the 12 May and 29 June 1966 (probable) Communist Chinese border violations, the CSAF directed that dynamic and aggressive efforts be made to obtain better control of USAF forces operating over North Vietnam. With United States' national interest also requiring this improved control, USAF officials believed the best method of achieving it was through a unilateral U.S. control facility. Given the responsibility of precluding violations of international boundaries, it would also enhance effectiveness of combat air operations. [49]

As a first step toward accomplishment of this goal, a small control room was established within the operations room at the Da Nang Control and Reporting Center (CRC). This secure location allowed receipt and limited plotting of Air Force Eyes Only data. 50/

Concurrent with its installation, a four-phased plan, Project Combat Lightning, was developed to substantially improve this control facility, since its space and communications limitations severely curtailed operational capability at the Da Nang CRC. Planning was evolved as follows: 51/

Phase I -- Improve interim facility at Da Nang CRC.

Phase II -- Provide a separate facility located adjacent to the Da Nang CRC.

Phase III -- Convert the system from manual to a semiautomatic operation in 1967.

Phase IV -- Improve the Phase III system and provide the 7AF Commander with additional control capabilities.

The Phase II facility of Project Combat Lightning became operational on 3 November 1966. It was configured from a mobile tactical air control package. Although it was an improvement over the Phase I facility, it still had the inherent limitations of a manual system. This facility was designated the Tactical Air Control Center-North Sector (TACC-NS). 52/

During 1966, preparations were under way for a semiautomatic system. The systems management agency, ESD, and Philco Corporation had completed in 1966, the initial site surveys at Da Nang, RVN, and at Udorn, Thailand, so that computerized systems could be installed there. By the end of 1966, building designs, cost estimates, and a computer program were being developed by these agencies. Phase III, designated as Project Seek Dawn, was scheduled to become operational on 15 June 1967. 53/

In early October, 7AF stated that there was an urgent requirement for authority to allow ECM aircraft to maneuver in the buffer zone in Route Packages 5 and 6A. PACAF, a little earlier, had reiterated CINCPAC's view that future violations of the CHICOM border could lead to cancellation or undesirable modification of the ROLLING THUNDER program. CINCPAC said that he would rather stop flying sorties in the northeast area than not to have assurance of elimination of violations. Accordingly, CINCPACAF on 7 October 1966, told 7AF that he recognized the advantages that would accrue from relaxation of the buffer zone restrictions. He noted, however, that the time was inopportune to press for such a relaxation, because of the increased sensitivity on the subject. 54/

Bombing Standdowns

The bombing standdowns at the beginning of 1965 and ending of 1965 were restrictive measures that mitigated effective air operations. These cease-fires were strenuously opposed by military authorities who contended that the enemy used these pauses to realign and strengthen his position. However, political considerations overruled these objectives. 55/

A North Vietnam bombing pause became effective on 24 December 1965, and lasted until 31 January 1966. (Blue Tree, Blue Springs, and Trojan Horse operations, however, continued.) At this time, the United States' "peace offensive" for solution of the Vietnam problem permeated the 56/

political and military atmosphere--not only in Vietnam, but on a worldwide scale. Fruition of this peaceful solution and its alternatives, if no agreement could be reached, was deeply rooted in effects that airpower had on the battlefront, and on the political/psychological fronts throughout the world. 57/

One of the essential elements of the air campaign against North Vietnam had been designed to cause the DRV to halt their support of the insurgency in RVN. If the pressures of air attacks were removed, the principal force which would cause the enemy to negotiate was either reduced or eliminated. 58/

CINCPAC's attitude was that the U.S. should not permit this type of situation. He said, "Otherwise, the impact of one of the basic strength factors would be reversed. Such a reversal would mean that the political pressures against the U.S. air campaign would be serving to cause the U.S. forces to cease and desist in attacks against the aggressor."

Observing that the DRV had offered no positive response to indicate a conscientious desire to begin negotiations, CINCPAC disapproved continuation of the standdown in 1966. He advised the JCS on 4 January, that its extension would weaken the negotiating posture of the U.S. Without positive results being achieved at an early date, he believed it would only "erode their campaign."

CINCPAC also presented to the JCS certain observations which had been made by COMUSMACV pertinent to the standdown up to that time: 59/

"COMUSMACV had stated that there had been no evidence to date, which indicated that the cessation of attacks on the DRV had had any effect on the PAVN/Viet Cong operations in RVN. The Viet Cong/PAVN probably would utilize any increased flow of supplies and personnel arriving in the SVN as a result of the cessation of attacks. These would be used to improve their capability to conduct operations. Certain happenings had indicated a business-as-usual attitude toward operations by the enemy in the South. Viet Cong-initiated incidents had continued at a high rate. Viet Cong/PAVN buildups have been reported in the Quang Tri areas of the I Corps and around the Capital Military Region.

"There was no hard evidence, nor was there any firm indication of any increase in the DRV capability which was directly related to the ROLLING THUNDER standdown. Indications were, however, that the standdown was allowing NVN to return to normal operational procedures. These included daytime reconstruction and the use of LOCs. It was assumed that maximum effort was being made to effect the restoration of lines of communications. This would be particularly so of the Lao Cay - Hanoi rail line. It would also be true for the LOCs south from Hanoi to Dong Hoi. It was probable that MIG training had been stepped up because of the standdown."

COMUSMACV informed CINCPAC that there were dangers confronting the U.S. forces as a result of the buildup by the PAVN and Viet Cong forces during the bombing pause. CINCPAC indicated to the Chairman of the Joint Chiefs of Staff that he concurred with COMUSMACV's stand. He was concerned with the risk facing the U.S. forces particularly, in the I CTZ. CINCPAC observed that the Blue Tree reconnaissance effort not only uncovered lucrative and perishable targets, but also proved that the enemy had been moving traffic along all the LOCs. For these reasons, he recommended an end to the bombing pause, and that airstrikes against North Vietnam be resumed. He suggested that if, for political reasons, full resumption of bombing could not be made, strikes should be carried out in the southern area of NVN. 60/

Shortly thereafter, COMUSMACV was authorized to commence air operations over NVN on 31 January 1966 at 0001 hours, Saigon time. On that date, he informed his subordinate commands of this authorization, which was to be disseminated to personnel only on a need-to-know basis. He added that the RVNAF were not to be informed of the resumption, and that no announcement would be made, either prior to or after the strike, as to the number of sorties flown or the amount of ordnance expended. He desired that all forces assume a posture of alertness at that time, since he had indications that the resumption of strikes over NVN might be the signal for a violent reaction by the VC/PAVN forces against friendly forces or installations throughout South Vietnam. He directed that all measures would be taken to safeguard personnel and installations and that a quick and effective response would follow any Viet Cong-initiated action. 61/

With respect to the TET ceasefire elsewhere in SEA, on 6 January, CINCPAC provided COMUSMACV with a policy of operations. The period of standdown would commence on 21 January at 0001 hours, Saigon time, and end on 23 January at 2400 hours, Saigon time. 62/

The TET policy, as provided by CINCPAC for South Vietnam, included the following guidelines: 63/

- No military offensive operations would be initiated except as indicated.

- Full alert posture would be assumed, and all security precautions would be continued. Patrol activity, including Market Time, would be continued.

- Ready Reaction Forces would be prepared to respond immediately to any PAVN/Viet Cong initiative. As military prudence dictated, this response could include counterattack by US/Free World/ARVN forces.

- Contact would not be broken for forces in contact with PAVN/Viet Cong forces unless there was clear evidence that they were making an effort to withdraw, or until the operation concerned was otherwise concluded.

- No offensive air operations would be initiated in the RVN. Air and naval operations in support of ground forces which were in contact with PAVN/Viet Cong forces might be authorized by COMUSMACV, if considered necessary for the security of the US/ARVN/FWMA forces. ARC LIGHT could be requested through normal channels for this purpose.

- Throughout the period, intensive aerial reconnaissance would be conducted.

- Hamlets and villages, whenever possible, would be avoided in the conduct of operations to minimize the impact on the civilian population.

CINCPAC observed that the intent of these policy guidelines was to prepare the U.S., RVN, and Free World Military Assistance Forces to counter, as feasible, the PAVN and Viet Cong attacks with the full strength of all arms. The intent also was "to assure and secure their safety," and was aimed at minimizing the PAVN and Viet Cong military exploitation of the standdown during TET.

CINCPAC requested that Viet Cong/PAVN hostile acts be reported immediately and in full detail, as the possibility existed that the enemy might attack non-RVNAF forces, while avoiding attacks on RVNAF forces. In such a case, participation by the VNAF in any resultant defensive actions, should be arranged through prior coordination. 64/

The CINCPAC policy for North Vietnam provided that operations, as then authorized, would be continued for Blue Tree, Blue Springs and Trojan Horse. As required, Big Eye, Big Look and Silver Dawn would be continued over the Gulf of Tonkin. Other operations, such as ROLLING THUNDER, could be made only if authorized. 65/

The CINCPAC policy for Laos outlined that the current tempo of operations would be continued or reduced, as required, if ROLLING THUNDER operations were resumed. Overflight of South Vietnam was authorized, however, overflight of the DRV was not authorized unless the ROLLING THUNDER program were resumed. 66/

CINCPAC advised COMUSMACV on 9 January that there would be no offensive air operations initiated in South Vietnam, and no offensive strikes would be conducted from RVN bases into either Laos or SVN during the TET bombing pause. The launching of airstrikes in Laos from bases in South Vietnam could appear to be an offensive action within South Vietnam. On the other hand, however, FAC aircraft could be engaged to support operations in Laos, as they normally were being launched from more remote bases. CINCPAC concluded that the tempo of strike operations in Laos was such that it could be maintained during the TET period by using CVA and Thai-based aircraft, supported, as required, by FAC aircraft based in South Vietnam. 67/

COMUSMACV did not agree with CINCPAC's guideline and on 13 January, he recommended that it be changed to be compatible with the following: 68/

> "COMUSMACV would have the authority to launch in-country aircraft from remote bases such as Cam Ranh and Chu Lai, in the event that an especially lucrative target were discovered in Laos.
>
> "COMUSMACV would maintain a certain number of armed aircraft on air alert during the TET period. These aircraft would have jettison areas designated in unpopulated parts of South Vietnam, in order to provide cover for the above option."

COMUSMACV informed CINCPAC that the Joint General Staff (JGS) was issuing a Cease-Fire directive, which was entirely compatible with the guidance given to COMUSMACV by CINCPAC on 6 January. The period of the TET cease-fire, to be announced by the GVN, would be from 20 January, 1200 hours, to 23 January, 1200 hours. COMUSMACV observed that the GVN's period would start 12 hours later and would end 12 hours earlier than the period announced by the National Liberation Front, and he had issued similar instructions, following the GVN lead. He also informed CINCPAC that documents in his possession indicated that the Viet Cong would resume hostilities immediately upon the end of the cease-fire period. He pointed out that the enemy had done so at the end of the 1965 TET and the 1965 Christmas Truce.

Because of these indications, COMUSMACV felt that it would be prudent to have the resumption of military actions by the government start 12 hours prior to the end of the Viet Cong cease-fire period. In that way, interdiction, harassing fire, and offensive patrolling could be undertaken to protect outposts, district towns, and isolated units. COMUSMACV considered such a precaution essential, since the enemy had carried out mortar attacks and harassing small arms attacks in such areas at the end of the Christmas Truce. He noted that at the end of the Christmas Truce in 1965, an effort had been made to prove that the Viet Cong had broken the cease-fire, and recommended that this approach not be taken for the end of the TET period. 69/

CINCPAC informed the JCS on 15 January, that COMUSMACV was opposed to any extension of the TET truce beyond the period designated. 70/ After coordination of this matter, he recommended these guidelines: 71/

- Notification would be provided well in advance, should any extension be considered.

- Military action was to be resumed 12 hours in advance of the current Viet Cong-announced time for resumption of hostilities.

- There would be no extension of the truce period beyond the announced TET cease-fire period.

It was CINCPAC's belief that the Viet Cong would not risk continuing the cease-fire 12 hours beyond that announced by the GVN. He told the JCS that for the safety of U.S. forces, it was necessary that military action be resumed at the time as announced by the GVN for ending the cease-fire. Because of their experience with the 1965 Christmas extension, the Viet Cong would hope for a TET extension. He observed that given this opportunity, the enemy might take steps to fully exploit any such situation. CINCPAC's position was that the enemy could not be given such an advantage without risking possible serious consequences. A few days later the termination date of the TET cease-fire was changed to 23 January, 1800 hours, Saigon time, at CINCPAC's request. 72/

The Secretary of Defense provided his public guidance for the TET cease-fire period. He stated that should there be no resumption of FWMAF initiatives stemming from Viet Cong action during the period 20 January, 1200 hours, to 23 January, 1800 hours, Saigon time, the announcement of the resumption of regular military operations would then be made at a time considered most appropriate by the Mission Council. This announcement would include a resume of the incidents and resulting casualties which had occurred during the TET cease-fire period. The Secretary of Defense further suggested that the spokesman could indicate that resumption of military operations had followed hostile acts of the Viet Cong against the FWMAF and the people of South Vietnam, during and after the standdown. Moreover, the spokesman could add that these Viet Cong initiatives had required the resumption of activities to protect friendly forces and the noncombatant population. U.S. resumption of hostilities could also be explained with statements recalling hostile acts of the Viet Cong during the Christmas standdown. 73/

On 18 January 1966, COMUSMACV ordered the U.S. forces to cease fire, except in self-defense, for the period from noon on 20 January to 1800 hours, on 23 January. He said that the order was issued in keeping with the Vietnamese lunar New Year holiday. 74/

Several days after the close of the cease-fire, COMUSMACV reported to CINCPAC that the enemy had initiated a total of 106 incidents or violations of the truce, of which 77 were against the FWMAF and 29 against RVNAF units. He pointed out that the majority of incidents in the I and II Corps were directed against the FWMAF. The incidents in the III Corps were directed equally against the FWMAF and the RVN. In the IV Corps area, the incidents were predominantely against the Vietnamese. There was at least one Viet Cong-initiated incident reported in 24 of the 43 provinces, however, of the total 106 incidents, only two were significant. The first significant incident occurred on 21 January, when the Viet Cong attacked a platoon of the Korean Marine Brigade in the Phu Yen Province, killing six and wounding 16. The other significant incident came the next day when the Viet Cong opened fire on a U.S. patrol from the 101st Airborne Brigade about ten kilometers northwest of Tuy Hoa. [75/]

During the 48-hour Christmas standdown in 1966, the enemy in South Vietnam and NVN made maximum use of this period to carry out resupply activities. COMUSMACV had observed the day after Christmas that numerous reports had indicated significantly increased supply activity in South Vietnam. [76/] On 29 December, CINCPAC added that the most significant enemy logistic effort had been observed in the waterborne resupply effort in the Sea Dragon area. During the 48-hour period of the standdown, the sightings of watercraft had been considerable. [77/] CINCPAC observed that both the Viet Cong and the NVA had made a concerted effort to take maximum advantage of this period to initiate tactical deployment as well. The pause gave the enemy an opportunity to move his logistic requirements by road, railway, and inland waterways, in addition to the shipping which took place in the coastal Sea Dragon area.

It appeared to CINCPAC that the enemy had been able to move a significant amount of supplies and equipment into the DMZ and adjacent areas as a result of the standdown. The enemy also deployed his troops to positions which provided him a tactical opportunity to mass for attack. 78/ The enemy had gained such an opportunity on the night of 27 December, when he overran positions of a U.S. artillery battery in the Binh Dinh Province. 79/

Throughout Southeast Asia, the air activity had declined as a result of the Christmas standdown and the moratorium on strikes in North Vietnam. The decline, however, had not been pronounced, and in some cases was not really noticeable from a statistical standpoint. Major declines appeared to be in the combat support activities, particularly in helicopter tasks. The moratorium in DRV, combined with the emphasis on interdiction in Laos, had resulted in a dramatic shift upward in the number of sorties flown there. Surprisingly, despite the moratorium, the tonnage delivered by the USAF increased approximately ten percent, with out-of-country tonnage increasing by 74 percent because of the Laos activity. No strikes were made in the ROLLING THUNDER area from 31 December 1966 - 1 January 1967. 80/

The same basic instructions that had been applicable for the Christmas standdown were carried over and in effect during the period 30 December 1966, 2300 hours, through 1 January 1967, 2300 hours. Instructions had qualifications for that period included: 81/

- No RVN-based aircraft would be used in operations over Laos;

- The 388th TFW Korat would standdown for runway repairs;

- 8th TFW, Ubon would operate at less than normal rate

41

with 355th TFW, Takhli, operating at half strength;

- The 435th TFS, 23d TASS, 602d TFS, and A-26 aircraft would operate at normal rate;

- ABCCC were fragged as usual;

- Thai-based strike/VR/FAC aircraft would be fragged into Laos;

- RVN-based O-1s would be utilized in the TIGER HOUND/TALLY HO area;

- Navy sorties at 100 per day were to be flown into the STEEL TIGER area.

USAF Personnel Detainees

Early in the year, the question arose as to the position to be taken by USAF military personnel who were lost, detained, or otherwise isolated in areas controlled by the USSR, Communist China, or their satellites. [82]

On 12 January 1966, CINCPACAF quoted the November 1965 guideline pertinent to Peacetime Aerial Reconnaissance (PAR) crews operating in the SEA combat area. (They were subject to the provision of paragraph 4b contained in Headquarters USAF's letter of 7 May 1959.) [83] In this reference, the PAR crews, if apprehended, were authorized to: [84]

- State their desire to be returned to U.S. control.

- State that their entry was inadvertent.

- If queried further, divulge only such information as had been provided in a well considered and plausible cover story....

The instructions further provided that all other USAF aircrew personnel, who were operating in the Southeast Asia combat zone and who were subject to capture in the same area, would adhere strictly to the Code of Conduct and the Geneva Convention relative to the treatment of prisoners of war. [85]

CINCPACAF, after reviewing these procedures in November 1965, realized an apparent need for all aircrew personnel liable to capture in the same area to be subject to uniform instruction pertaining to their conduct as captives. At the time of the review, the Air Staff believed these provisions for the PAR crews should apply when they flew missions originating outside Southeast Asia, until they entered the combat zone. The Air Staff considered that only when the crews entered the combat zone, should they be subject to the same instructions as other non-PAR aircrew personnel. The review indicated that the cover stories, in this case, would still be authorized for PAR crews, if they were inadvertently downed in other areas; i.e., China. The review further stated that the combat zone would be limited to a precisely defined geographical area. [86]

After coordination with the 7AF Commander, CINCPACAF on 17 January 1966, replied to CSAF that he concurred with these procedures, except that the origin of the missions should not be a criterion for use of a cover story by downed crews. Furthermore, he told CSAF that he held the following view: [87]

> "...Crews downed in the combat zone must adhere to a strict code of conduct. PAR crews downed in other areas may use a cover story. Combat zone should be defined as Laos and North and South Vietnam and the territorial waters adjacent thereto...."

CHAPTER III

COMMAND AND CONTROL

Centralized Air Control

The 2d Air Division was redesignated Seventh Air Force (7AF) on 2 April 1966. COMUSMACV approved of this change, since this organization would remain a component, and there would be no significant increase in the size of the headquarters. Lt. Gen. William W. Momyer succeeded Lt. Gen. Joseph H. Moore as Commander, 7AF, and DEPCOMUSMACV for Air Operations on 1 July 1966. 1/

One of the critical issues discussed during 1966 was central control and management of all airpower. The Deputy Commander, 7AF, pointed out in his End of Tour Report, which covered the period 23 April 1965 - 1 August 1966, that the 7AF was a subordinate command of MACV, with command assignment over all USAF units based in South Vietnam. Tactical units stationed in Thailand were assigned to the Thirteenth Air Force in the Philippines, and were under operational control of 7AF. Marine Air Wings worked directly for Marine ground units and unless released by them, were not available for general use. The Navy provided three carriers, one of which operated in the Dixie station area; the other two operated from Yankee station against targets in North Vietnam, as directed by CINCPAC.

The Deputy Commander explained that in-country airlift was provided by Army Caribous on a unilateral basis; AF C-123s and C-130s were integrated

44

into the SEA airlift system under operational control of 7AF; and cargo and priority assignments were controlled by MACV J-4. Targets for B-52 strikes were developed by MACV with no inputs or evaluations by 7AF. Requirements generated by MACV for the Military Airlift Command (MAC) were established without consideration of the input of these operations on oversaturated airfields controlled and operated by 7AF. This was also true of Air America air operations in South Vietnam which competed for airfield facilities and air space but were not affiliated with any other service.

The Deputy Commander stated that although the 7AF Commander had been designated the DEPCOMUSMACV for Air Operations, in reality, he was essentially the Commander of Air Force activities. There was no single Air Commander in Vietnam and air resources were fragmented among various command agencies with no centralized control or direction. 2/

The Deputy Commander stated that COMUSMACV should have one Air Commander responsible to him for providing his total Air Force air support. In his opinion, all requirements for B-52s, intratheater, and MAC support should be handled in this manner. He believed that establishment of a single Air Force contact would be a major step toward elimination of many problems which had developed because of insufficient coordination due to involvement of many commands. 3/

The Deputy Commander's End of Tour Report cited that the present composition of MACV Headquarters made it a Joint Headquarters in name only. The Air Force did not have proper representation on the staff, commensurate with the contribution it was making in the war. COMUSMACV had no intention of correcting this situation, until the Air Force was willing to place all air resources involved in the war under his command. These would include the fighters operating from Thailand bases and the C-130s operating from the Pacific base area. It was recognized that such an assignment of forces raised serious questions as to their availability to meet other contingency war plans. Such a war might or might not occur but in the meantime, the Air Force stood to lose a good deal of stature with the Army for not joining the "team." Even more important, the Deputy Commander pointed out that confusion existed within the Air Force structure when unorthodox command arrangements were established. 4/

Because of these reasons, the Deputy Commander made the following recommendations: 5/

- Assign all tactical airlift resources operating in Vietnam to the 7AF as presently provided for in Air Force Doctrine.

- Place the 3d Air Division in Guam under operational control of Seventh Air Force.

- Press COMUSMACV to establish a true Joint Headquarters and place all 7AF assets under his command, including Thailand-based forces.

In October 1966, four months after assuming command of the 7AF, the new commander stated he was convinced that the only real solution to the problem of coordinating all air operations was to place them under his operational control. He stated that failure to make this change would have a serious and adverse effect on the employment, command and control, and

46

long-range assessment of the utilization of strategic airpower in a theater of operations. [6]

Reemphasizing this theme, he commented on another occasion that: [7]

> "...The air component should be a single point of authority for MACV on all air matters...The most inherent weakness in the air command structure today is the absence of an air component command having authority and control over all air matters in his assigned area of responsibility...."

The position of the 7AF continued to center around two cardinal issues in providing the most effective air support to COMUSMACV: (1) control of air should be vested in a single air commander; and (2) existing controls and procedures were adequate to apply the air forces available in accordance with the tactical and strategic considerations. [8] (See Project CHECO SEA Report, "Control of Air Strikes in SEA 1961-1966.")

Airstrikes Review Board

A MACV Board of Officers was established on 26 January 1966, with the DCS/Operations, 7AF, appointed Chairman of the Board. Its purpose was to review current and projected airstrike programs; its function was to recommend measures which would insure optimum sortie effectiveness. [9]

In explaining reasons for the formation of this Board, the MACV, Chief of Staff stated that employment of airstrike resources in association with in-country operations, as well as the ROLLING THUNDER, STEEL TIGER, TIGER HOUND and BARREL ROLL operations had generated a need for major sortie requirements. Effective utilization of airstrike resources for in-country,

Thailand, and carrier-based fighters, demanded that a continuing assessment of priorities be made. 10/ This required a continuing assessment of the allocation of effort, along with target criteria, and results achieved. Shortages of certain categories of air ordnance required careful and continuing assessment of ordnance selection, weight of expenditure, and its effects. This was mandatory in the interest of economy of resources and optimum sortie effectiveness. In view of this necessity, the scope of the Board's activity included: 11/

- Analysis of sorties and air ordnance requirements versus capabilities.

- Evaluation of procedures addressed to the management of the airstrike effort and the formulation of proposals designed to insure maximum sortie effectiveness and optimum utilization of air ordnance.

- Review and modification of target criteria, as necessary.

- Study of the effects of weather on sortie allocation and effectiveness and development of recommendations pertaining to this matter as appropriate.

- The handling of such related inquiries as deemed necessary by the Board.

On 7 May 1966, MACV instructed the 7AF Commander to establish contingency plans and procedures, which would permit rapid and effective control of total airstrike assets by the 7AF in the event of an operational emergency. The plans were to be submitted to MACV by 15 June 1966. 12/

On 19 May 1966, the 7AF informed PACAF that it was preparing a proposed

MACV OPLAN to document existing procedures to assume operational control by the 7AF Commander of total strike assets in the event of a MACV operational emergency. The 7AF observed that introduction of I MAW and Navy airstrike assets into the TACS would continue through the in-country TACC. The request for close air support for the III MAF would be introduced into the JAGO at I Corps and DASC and would abide by established procedures being utilized for other friendly ground forces in South Vietnam.

The 7AF also informed PACAF that assumption of operational command of total airstrike assets of I MAW and the Navy could be accommodated within existing 7AF Command and Control procedures and equipment. PACAF was told that COMUSMACV and his staff had been briefed on equipment and the concept of operations, which were planned for present and future adverse weather operations in SEA. [13]

These data, plus a briefing on requirements, procedures, and special operations were to be furnished the Navy Liaison Officer (NAVLO). The NAVAIR operation was limited by such factors as deck cycling, rough seas, and light ordnance loads with catapult operations. For this reason, utilization of these air assets had been primarily in preplanned operations, as full dependence on NAVAIR would require that requests for sorties for CAS had to be met. They added that necessary operational accommodations to meet immediate and fleeting target requirements of tactical operations would be required from carrier forces. 7AF was proceeding with preparations for the formulation of a draft operational plan. [14]

49

At a meeting held on 26 May 1966, representatives from USMACV, USAF (7AF), USN (Seventh Fleet, NAVLO) and USMC discussed this matter. The 7AF Commander observed that agreement had been completed on the contents of the proposed MACV OPLAN. 7AF's position was that in an emergency designated by COMUSMACV, all U.S. strike assets would be controlled through the SVN Tactical Air Control System; and would be under the operational control of the Seventh Air Force. 15/

ARC LIGHT Program Control

With respect to the ARC LIGHT (B-52) program, MACV selected and designated targets. MACV also determined forces required and requested them directly and without regard to air resources in SVN. The Commander, 7AF, contended that target approval and recommendation (control) for utilization of SAC strikes should be vested in him. 16/

As the 7AF Director of Intelligence pointed out, this system effectively eliminated 7AF from participation in target development, selection of ordnance, fuzing, selection of tactics, and from any say-so at all, as to whether the B-52 was the optimum weapon systems for the target in the first place. Weapon systems, ordnance, and targets must be matched for optimum cost effectiveness. For example, an area target containing a VC concentration which received warning might be hit best by a force that maintained its presence over the target for a sustained period, as opposed to a one-time massive attack where the enemy had taken cover. These choices should be available to the commander requesting target destruction, an option not currently available. If the B-52 force committed to conventional bombing in SEA were placed in the Tactical Air Control System, then 7th AF, with its targeting and tactics staffs (augmented with ground force liaison personnel, if desired), could provide optional forces optimized for the task. The Intelligence Director pointed out that the foregoing also applied to support of Marine ground forces who were currently requesting B-52 strikes without trying 7AF tactical forces on the job. 17/

In September 1966, the 7AF Commander recommended to USAF that he be given operational control of the B-52 forces during the execution phase. This would in no way hinder the selection of targets by MACV which, he said, would continue to remain within the purview of MACV's responsibility. 18/

Headquarters, USAF, advised the 7AF Commander that should control of B-52 operations be passed to the Air Component Commander, a SAC ADVON would be provided to do the operational planning. This would satisfy the requirement to streamline and improve the targeting, tasking, approval, and coordination procedures as they pertained to the B-52 operations through counsel of the Air Deputy. At the same time, this arrangement would provide better integration of the ARC LIGHT program into the overall SEA air operations, and would insure that qualified personnel made the force allocation; i.e., the determination of whether strategic or tactical forces attacked a specific target. 19/

On 21 December 1966, the JCS proposed that SACLO become a SAC ADVON attached to the DEPCOMUSMACV for Air Operations, and on 26 December,

COMUSMACV concurred in this proposal.[20] He pointed out, however, that the function of planning and coordinating strike requests to the SAC ADVON would be retained in the ACofS, J-3 (COC), MACV.[21] On 6 January 1967, JCS requested that the SAC ADVON concept be implemented as mutually agreeable to CINCPAC and CINCSAC.[22]

On 10 January 1967, the 7AF obtained COMUSMACV's approval of transferring the operational planning function for the ARC LIGHT program from MACV COC to a SAC ADVON, which would be deployed to the Tan Son Nhut Air Base, to operate under cognizance of the DEPCOMUSMACV for Air Operations.[23]

Route Package Assignments - North Vietnam

A command anomaly was generated through the assignment of geographic areas in NVN between the Air Force and Navy. This development came about through continuing pressure by the Navy for geographic assignment of areas in NVN on a permanent basis. Initially this procedure had been agreed upon as a time-cycling arrangement, so as to prevent Air Force and Navy forces from being in the same area at the same time. This, in turn, was followed by the Route Package plan with a change every two weeks coinciding with the ROLLING THUNDER periods. In early 1966, it was decided to use the same Route Package plan, changing every 30 days under the existing concept of ROLLING THUNDER. This system was modified later as a result of a CINCPAC decision to assign permanent geographic areas between the Air Force and the Navy in consonance with the latter's request.[24]

The Air Force Deputy for Operations pointed out that the CINCPAC

assignment of geographic areas was impractical. It ignored the assets
which the Air Force had built up to do the total air job in NVN. It did not
treat the vital subject of targeting as related to a carefully integrated
air plan. The Navy could not provide the same kind of reconnaissance coverage as the Air Force, either in quality or quantity, resulting in an obvious
degradation of intelligence information in Route Packages 2, 3, 4, and 6
in NVN. [25/]

Despite the 7AF efforts, the Route Package system continued throughout the year. By the end of 1966, the Air Force controlled Route Packages
1, 5, and 6A, while the Navy continued to control operations in Route Packages 2, 3, 4, and 6B. [26/] The 7AF assets could be used with common concurrence
in the Navy Route Package areas. [27/]

ABCCC

Until September 1965, when one Airborne Battlefield Command and Control
Center (ABCCC) was made available for Project South Shores, there had been
no aircraft deployed to SEA, which was adequately equipped to function as
an efficient airborne command post. By the end of the year, there were
four ABCCCs operating in SEA. The ABCCC had been designed as a command
control and communications compartment. It was capable of airborne operations when installed in a C-130E aircraft and for ground operations when
removed from the aircraft. The compartment contained UHF, VHF, and HF radios
and was capable of both voice and TTY communications. When airborne, it
had an automatic radio relay capability. It was capable of operating in a
tactical environment as a TACC, DASC, alternate CRC, a coordination facility

for SAC and other special missions. It could also act as an airborne command and control facility for the Joint Task Force operations.[28]

CHAPTER IV

FRIENDLY AIR CAPABILITIES

Mission

The Commander, 7AF, was tasked with supporting the U.S. national objective in SEA through the use of Air Force resources by conducting air operations in the Republic of Vietnam, Laos, and North Vietnam. His assigned mission was as follows: [1]

- To maintain the assigned and attached force at a degree of combat readiness that would insure the success of Headquarters PACAF-directed military operations.

- To function as the Air Force component commander for the U.S. Military Assistance Command, Vietnam (USMACV) and the U.S. Military Assistance Command, Thailand (USMACTHAI).

- To advise COMUSMACV on all matters pertaining to effective employment of tactical air support in the Republic of Vietnam.

- To advise and assist the Vietnamese Air Force (VNAF) in achieving a state of combat readiness.

Strength and Deployment

To accomplish these objectives, the USAF greatly expanded its manpower and materiel resources during the year. At the beginning of 1966, tactical aircraft resources under operational control of 7AF consisted of 780 fixed and rotary wing aircraft (599 in RVN and 181 in Thailand). They were assigned as follows: Offensive missions--388; reconnaissance--60; special air warfare--33; air defense--12; airlift--89; support operations--198. These aircraft were deployed in 96 organizational units: 50 assigned, 33 attached, and 13 units on temporary duty status. In addition, other USAF organizational units out-of-country provided mission support and airlift into RVN as required. The B-52 daily bombing sorties out of Guam (SAC-3d AD), airlift out of Japan, Okinawa, and the Philippines (MAC), and field tests of tactical air operational prototype weapons systems (TAC/AFSC) were continuing at a stepped-up pace. 2/

By the end of the year, the 7AF possessed 1,234 operationally controlled aircraft, an increase of 454 over those possessed at the beginning of the year. With 834 aircraft possessed in-country and 400 in Thailand, this represented the largest fleet to that time. Of the total 1,234 operationally controlled USAF aircraft in SEA, slightly more than 51 percent (633) were offensive aircraft, while support aircraft accounted for approximately 23 percent (285). Reconnaissance type aircraft accounted for approximately 11 percent (141), airlift, 10 percent (119), special warfare 3 percent (34), and defense, 2 percent (22). 3/

Air Force strength more than doubled during 1966, from an assigned total of 19,000 personnel in January 1966, to 42,378 in December 1966. At the end of the year, only two bases (Tan Son Nhut and Phan Rang) were more than 100 percent manned in officer assignments. Tan Son Nhut had 1,702 officers authorized and 2,385 assigned; Phan Rang had 243 authorized and 289 assigned. Cam Ranh Bay, Pleiku, Qui Nhon, and Tuy Hoa were the only bases where airmen strength was lower than authorized. Tan Son Nhut had 2,417 assigned over and above the authorized strength. 4/

After an assessment of logistical capabilities, in which the Secretary of Defense (SECDEF) participated on 28 November in RVN, COMUSMACV, in December, reviewed the limited tactical air base support program for Vietnam and concurred with CINCPAC's proposal to reduce the number of tactical fighter squadrons required by the end of 1966, from 30 to 23. COMUSMACV recommended, however, that 17 USAF and six USMC jet strike squadron-equivalents be deployed in-country, with the provision that one aircraft carrier (CVA) continue on Dixie station for in-country strike support, until sufficient land-based aircraft were in-country to meet SVN strike requirements. 5/

The 7AF calendar year (CY) 1966 deployment requirements were programmed in Honolulu during a joint-service conference held during 17 January - 6 February 1966. Aircraft requirements were matched against the best estimates of USAF capabilities to meet COMUSMACV needs and dates. 6/

During the conference, COMUSMACV emphasized to CINCPAC the close and important relationship which pertained to availability of airfields, ports, and RVN deployments. His revaluation, based on projected CY 1966 strike sortie rates, had confirmed the requirements for three additional jet air bases in RVN.

Tuy Hoa constituted an agreed site, and preliminary surveys were conducted to determine additional suitable construction sites. They resulted in the nomination of a site on the Qui Nhon Peninsula, and another at Phu Bai airfield as preferred locations. It was desirable that construction economy and security be attained by satelliting the new Qui Nhon airfield on the port. Conversely, capabilities of the port would extend to a wider range of forces and activities. It was clear that a port facility was required at, or near, Hue in connection with the Phu Bai airfield to support USAF operations.

Port considerations associated with the Tuy Hoa airfield were solely for support of the air base and its security force. This factor, plus uncertainties affecting completion of a usable port at Tuy Hoa, prior to the monsoon season in 1966, caused construction to be postponed. Commencing in April, efforts were reoriented toward construction at Qui Nhon or Hue/Phu Bai. Concurrently, COMUSMACV studied the expansion of existing jet air bases to absorb 1966 programmed fighter squadrons. By 1 March, a new program would encompass all required new sites and the expansion of existing bases to accommodate tactical jet aircraft deployment to RVN. 7/

The conference closed on 6 February, having established U.S. forces and logistic support required for RVN, to include monthly sortie rates for air operations in SEA by tactical strike aircraft and B-52 ARC LIGHT bomber forces. Strike sortie rates were keyed to available munitions estimated from February through December 1966. ARC LIGHT operations would continue at 400 sorties per month, which would increase to 450 on 1 April, 600 on 1 July, and continue at that level through 1966. Tactical fighter sorties would maintain an average of 150 sorties per month per US/FWMAF forces in-country maneuver battalion. A total of 7,800 sorties per month would support the RVNAF. Additionally, 3,000 sorties per month were marked for Laos and

7,100-7,500 were allocated for NVN. COMUSMACV could direct additional sorties from in-country assets when improved targeting in Laos indicated a higher priority.[8/] Based on these established sortie rates, the CY 1966 deployment buildup of jet tactical fighter squadrons was programmed to total 28 in RVN (18 USAF, 10 USMC), and 11 tactical fighter squadrons in Thailand.

Phase II, II-A, and II-A (revised) USAF deployments in 1966, were scheduled as follows: two tactical fighter squadrons to Phan Rang AB in April, one in May, and the fourth in November; one tactical fighter squadron to Bien Hoa AB in July, and another in August; three tactical fighter squadrons to Qui Nhon AB in July, and the fourth in November. Four reconnaissance aircraft would be deployed to Tan Son Nhut AB in July, followed by a tactical reconnaissance squadron in August 1966.[9/]

Makeshift beddown arrangements at alternate air bases permitted the arrival in-country of some deferred Phase I (1965) squadrons. On 5 January, 25 A-1Es of the 1st Air Commando Squadron moved from Bien Hoa to Pleiku, thereby permitting a F-100 squadron from CONUS to move into Bien Hoa on 1 February. This first step toward "making ramp space available for jets" relocated USAF conventional strike aircraft from Bien Hoa, leaving only VNAF A-1s and USAF F-100s. Shifting was completed when the 602d USAF Commando Fighter Squadron (A-1Es) moved to Nha Trang early in February.

In other makeshifts, the first F-4C squadron (391st) of the 366th Tactical Fighter Wing, scheduled to be based at Phan Rang, was temporarily placed at Cam Ranh Bay on 31 January. An advance party of the wing moved into Phan Rang facilities; one additional F-4C squadron (391st) deployed into Da Nang. By 14 March, both squadrons plus a third F-4C (389th) squadron from CONUS moved into Phan Rang. This move completed the Phase I squadron deployments to RVN. Efforts to schedule a firm beddown for Phase I-A tactical jet squadrons, programmed for RVN and Thailand, were complicated by the lack of airfield availability and the saturation of ramp facilities. 10/

In April, CINCPAC recomputed SEA TFS and monthly sortie requirements based on a JCS revised schedule of maneuver battalion deployments. It was clear that previous estimates of combat sorties would necessarily change to account for sharply increased detection of infiltration targets in Laos and North Vietnam. About 80 percent of the Laos/NVN combat sorties flown by 1 April were in the attack category. Accordingly, the programmed 10,000 per month combat sortie rate for 1966 was revised upward to 12,400 for Laos and NVN. Projected in-country monthly sortie requirements for 1966, gradually increased from 17,190 in April, to 22,490 in December. Tactical fighter squadrons required to meet this task in 1966 were reprogrammed. 11/

In the meantime, JCS recommended to the SECDEF, a revised deployment program for 1966, comprised of 20 squadrons in RVN and 11 squadrons in Thailand, based on the USAF capability to meet CINCPAC/COMUSMACV stated needs (May - December 1966) for 11 tactical fighter squadrons. To meet the requirement for 11 squadrons, it was necessary for the JCS to include one F-104 TFS in the tactical fighter role and one F-102 FIS for the air defense mission at Da Nang. 12/

CINCPAC's request for comments on the new JCS-recommended deployment program brought immediate response from the COMUSMACV, CINCPACAF, and CINCPACFLT. Based on consideration of the positions held by component commanders, CINCPAC, on 20 April, requested JCS' concurrence in the following revised TFS/FIS deployments for closure in SEA during 1966: [13/]

SEA DEPLOYMENTS--APRIL-DECEMBER 1966

UNIT	TYPE	CLOSURE	BASE	SOURCE
1 TFS	F-5	Apr	Bien Hoa, RVN	SVN
2 TFS	F-100	May	Phan Rang, RVN	PACOM & CONUS
2 TFS	F-105	May	Korat, Thailand	PACOM
6 Acft*	F-102	Jun	Da Nang, RVN	CLARK AB
1 TFS	F-100	Jul	Phan Rang, RVN	CONUS
1 TFS**	F-104	Jul	Udorn, Thailand	CONUS
1 TFS	F-100	Sep	Phan Rang, RVN	CONUS
2 TFS	F-100	Nov	Qui Nhon, RVN	CONUS
1 FIS	F-102	Jun	Clark AB, PI	CONUS

* Staged to Da Nang from parent squadron based at Clark AB.

** Replaced F-4C squadron at Udorn, scheduled to move to Ubon.

TACTICAL STRIKE SQUADRONS IN SEA BY MONTH

1966:	Apr	May	Jun	Jul	Aug	Sep	Oct	Nov	Dec
SVN:	20	22	23	25	25	28	28	30	30
USAF: #	13	15	16	17	17	18	18	20	20
##	(12)	(14)	(16)	(16)	(17)	(17)	(18)	(18)	(20)
USMC:	7	7	7	8	8	10	10	10	10
THAILAND:	8	10	10	11	11	11	11	11	11
TOTAL SEA:	28	32	33	36	36	39	39	41	41

\#   Air defense F-4C squadron at Da Nang was not included until relieved by F-102 detachment in June.

\#\#   JCS schedule recommended to SECDEF, 4 Apr 66.

Combat sorties required versus the total tactical fighter strike capability provided under CINCPAC's adjusted tactical strike aircraft deployment plan would produce a net deficit of 2,000 sorties in April, but projected an even score by June and a plus score in August and December. The SECDEF approved the CINCPAC plan on 30 April 1966, and PACOM's Phase II-A (revised) program document was revised accordingly. 14/

By 30 April, 12 tactical jet fighter squadrons were in place at five RVN bases and seven, of eight jet fighter squadrons due in Thailand, were in place. (One F-105 squadron from PACOM was deferred until early May.) Two tactical reconnaissance squadrons (RF-4C and RF-101s) and one F-102 FIS, plus an F-5 TFS at Bien Hoa and a B-57 TRS at Da Nang, completed the April unit inventory of USAF strike aircraft. 15/

During the Honolulu Planning Conference (May - June 1966), tactical air support requirements were determined on the basis of maneuver battalions requiring sorties beginning the month after their arrival. Sorties required for support of in-country ground forces were computed at five sorties per day per U.S. Army/FWMA forces. Sortie support for US/FWMA Marine forces was increased by one-third due to composition of their maneuver battalions. 16/

Out-of-country sortie allocations were based on the continuing requirement of 5,000 sorties per month in Laos, and 11,200 sorties per month in NVN. Restrictions at that time limited implementation of the CINCPAC concept for striking NVN POL, ports, and power plants. A marked increase was required in those air programs designed to reduce the flow of men and materials into SVN. The requirement existed to build up a sortie capability as rapidly as possible to reach the desired level of 11,200 sorties per month in NVN.

There were elements of capability inherent in these sortie allocations, since the rapidity of the SVN buildup had to a certain degree been factored by judgment as to what was practical and feasible in terms of new tactical fighter squadrons introduced into SVN and Thailand. Ordnance limitations and construction requirements were taken into consideration. Addition of a sixth CVA in SEA would also permit a more rapid buildup in sortie allocations for the NVN air campaign commencing in January 1967. Tactical fighter squadron capabilities were based on: (1) SVN-based squadrons at the sortie rate of 1.1 combat sortie per day for squadron unit equipment (UE); and (2) Thai-based squadrons at a sortie rate of 1.8 combat sorties per day for squadron UE. 17/

Two USAF A-1 squadrons produced 1,800 combat sorties per month based on the assumption that the squadron aircraft UE would be maintained throughout CY 1967. Six VNAF A-1 squadrons, also computed at their UE of 1.8 combat sorties per day per aircraft, accounted for 3,600 combat sorties per month based on the assumption that the squadron aircraft UE would be maintained, or equivalent sorties would be produced, throughout CY 1967. CVA capabilities were based on: (1) 3,000 combat sorties per month per in-country CVA (except USS INTREPID--limited to 2,600 combat sorties); (2) 2,400 combat sorties per month per out-of-country CVA; and (3) a sixth CVA in SEA would produce 1,440 combat sorties per month when operating from Yankee Station, based on 18 operating days per month. [18]

During July, Phan Rang AB received two F-100 squadrons: the 612th TFS and the 615th TFS--the first F-100 squadrons to deploy to Phan Rang. Meanwhile, Udorn AB, Thailand, received the final increment of F-104s of the 435th TFS and ten RF-4Cs for the 611th Tactical Reconnaissance Squadron (TRS). These were the first RF-4Cs to deploy to Thailand, with the remaining 14 scheduled for arrival in September. [19]

CINCPAC raised the question in July of using Thai-based U.S. aircraft to support military operations in SVN in the event of massive VC/NVA force attacks during the monsoon season. The American Embassy, Bangkok, without benefit of a direct reply from the Thai Prime Minister, concluded that no difficulty was foreseen in gaining permission on a case-by-case basis, if sufficient advance warning with justification, including intelligence, was available. Should an emergency situation dictate the use of Thai-based aircraft to support RVN operations, COMUSMACV and the Commander, 7AF, in coordination with COMUSMACTHAI, would provide the Ambassador with a detailed briefing concerning the situation in SVN and projected employment of U.S. aircraft from Thai bases.[20]

Meanwhile, COMUSMACV notified the Commander, 7AF, on 30 July, that DIXIE CVA was scheduled to move immediately by order of CINCPAC to Yankee Station. COMPACFLT would maintain three CVAs in the vicinity of Yankee Station, and assume responsibility for strike areas in the vicinity of Nape and Barthelemy Passes. The 7AF would take action to adjust in-country air effort and realignment of mission responsibility. The JCS on 2 August requested CINCPAC's revision by 7 October, of sortie and munitions plans resulting from realignment of the CVA.[21]

On 5 August 1966, CINCPACAF notified CINCPAC of a 7AF proposal, which had COMUSMACV concurrence, to move the 8th Tactical Bomber Squadron (B-57s) from Da Nang to Phan Rang. It would be replaced with the Phan Rang-based 366th TFW Headquarters and the 389th TFS (F-4Cs), about 30 September 1966. An additional F-4C TFS at Da Nang would complement use of Ubon's F4Cs and Udorn's F-104s, in their escort role during larger scale NVN operations.

Consolidation of similar aircraft at Da Nang provided better strike sortie support (B-57s) to IV CTZ, since the CVA was unavailable at Dixie Station. Furthermore, the 366th TFW had been trained principally in F-4C operations--the parent wing of three F-4C squadrons originally destined for Phan Rang.

Relocation of the 389th TFS offered better use of F-4Cs in NVN and Laos, because the unrefueled action radius of these aircraft from Da Nang permitted striking most of the current targets in those areas. It improved response time, offered more expedient scheduling, greater tactical flexibility, and a more resourceful operational posture.

Accordingly, on 19 August 1966, CINCPAC approved relocation of these tactical units as proposed by 7AF.[22/] During this month, also, the 352d TFS arrived at Phan Rang, bringing the TFS strength to one F-4C and three F-100 squadrons. Movement of the 614th TFS (F-100s) into Phan Rang during September, would complete TFS deployments to SEA for CY 1966.[23/]

The possibility of introducing FWMAF air units to augment air operations, and permit the release of some USAF resources in RVN for other commitments was under consideration during 1966. By the end of the year, however, the only firm commitment was the move of eight Royal Australian Air Force (RAAF) Canberra (B-57) aircraft to South Vietnam.[24/]

Vietnamese Air Force (VNAF)

The Vietnamese Air Force (VNAF), under the active command of the Prime Minister of South Vietnam, Air Vice Marshal Nguyen Cao Ky, continued to lend its support to air operations. Ky, by retaining control of the Air Force, where he had a loyal following, was able to secure military and political support to carry out his dual role. Col. Tran Van Minh, the Deputy Commander, provided the VNAF staff and subordinate units with the strong, daily leadership they needed.[25/]

The combat capability and effectiveness of the VNAF gradually, but consistently improved during 1966. The number of hours flown increased by approximately 23 percent to 19,389 hours, and the number of sorties flown increased by approximately 34 percent to 12,938 in December. The VNAF flew approximately 24 percent of the total USAF and VNAF sorties in South Vietnam during the year. The tonnage of munitions delivered increased and mission results were gratifying. These noticeable improvements were the direct result of general betterment of aircraft utilization, the Not Operational Ready, Supply (NORS) rate being below the five percent standard, except for helicopters, and the Not Operational Ready Maintenance (NORM) rate being below the standard of 24 percent. 26/

The VNAF experienced rapid expansion from 1962 to 1965, but after the direct commitment of the USAF in Vietnam, there was no need for major expansion, since U.S. forces could absorb additional requirements of the conflict. Its major task became one of stabilization, professionalization, and modernization. The VNAF was now comparable to a numbered U.S. Tactical Air Force, but it was tailored to the counterinsurgency role. The tactical wings, one in each of the four CTZs, were organized, so that they could support ground forces, provide a visual reconnaissance and psychological warfare capability, liaison control of fighter squadron strikes and, with helicopter squadrons, medical evacuation, and a resupply capability. 27/

In late 1965, COMUSMACV had directed the establishment of a Tactical Air Control System (TACS) for command and control of USAF/VNAF aircraft and for coordination of USMC/USN airstrikes under USMACV control. The

67

TACS was to be used as an operational and training vehicle. Allocation and control of USAF/VNAF air resources and coordination of USMC/USN aircraft would be exercised through the elements of this system.

Aircraft and units operating under the TACS would be allocated through the Tactical Air Control Center (TACC) to Direct Air Support Centers (DASC) as appropriate for operations in support of CTZs. U.S. Army aviation assets would be allocated as directed by COMUSMACV. USAF and VNAF resources were subject to reallocation, recall, or diversion through the TACC. The Commander, 7AF, in his capacity as MACV Air Force Component Commander, would: (1) coordinate all U.S. air operations and VNAF activities necessary in conducting an active air defense; (2) establish and operate, in conjunction with the RVNAF, a TACS for command and control of USAF/VNAF strike aircraft; and (3) provide essential training for VNAF in offensive and defensive tactical air operations. [28]

VNAF's assigned strength increased from 13,500 in January 1966, to 15,521 by the end of the year, while the authorized strength increased from 15,563 to 16,490. With this increase, the VNAF personnel posture improved. The desertion rate dropped to an average of 20 deserters monthly and was expected to be reduced further, as more severe punishment was meted to military absent without leave. Even now, VNAF had the lowest desertion rate of all the armed forces, 3.5 per 1,000 assigned. Great strides were made in formal and on-the-job training, and greater emphasis was placed on psychological operations and civic action. The shortage of pilots continued to be a problem, but waivers were requested and received for weight and height requirements. Some relief in this problem area was anticipated, providing the VNAF took advantage of these waivers. [29]

Since the VNAF was in a transitional phase from conventional to jet aircraft, pilot training requirements in support of this program were high and would remain so for several years, even without considering combat losses. It was therefore important that in-country pilot training be accomplished at the maximum rate. Normal in-country production of VNAF pilots had been 40 per year, but to provide a continuous flow of U-17 pilots to the field, a minimum of 90-100 pilots per year was needed. [30]

At the beginning of 1966, the VNAF had a total of 396 assigned aircraft including A-1G/Hs, H-34s, O-1As, U-17As, U-6As, C-47s, RC-47s and an EC-47. As of 31 December 1966, the total assigned aircraft were 357, with 403 authorized. Because of an A-1 aircraft shortage for U.S. forces, it was decided to replace VNAF A-1s with substitute aircraft, and to use VNAF A-1s to cover USN and USAF A-1 attrition. CINCPAC suggested that F-5s and other related aircraft be procured for the VNAF to replace A-1s.

On 6 July, the Air Force Advisory Group (AFAG) concurred that six VNAF A-1 squadrons should be converted to two F-5 and four AT-37 jet aircraft. In November, there were radical changes to the VNAF F-5 modernization program. The JCS, CINCPAC and the SECDEF approved for VNAF one 18 UE F-5, three 18 UE AT-37, and two 18 UE A-1 squadrons. This represented a considerable slowdown from previous plans. The new proposal was acceptable to the USAF, if the phasedown of A-1 Squadrons from the current 25 UE to 18 was expedited. This compromise would accomplish some VNAF modernization and also help alleviate the A-1 shortage for U.S. forces.

The shortage of H-34 helicopters was another problem that commanded attention during the year. The shortage had a direct impact on the lift capability available to U.S. forces, with a corresponding increase in requirements for U.S. helicopter support for RVNAF. The CSAF informed CINCPAC on 21 September that JCS had approved a total of 39 H-34s, which were to arrive in South Vietnam by the end of Fiscal Year 1967. The introduction of modernization plans concurrently with the effort to bring the helicopter program up to authorized strength presented another complicated factor. [31]

The VNAF accident rate continued to be a matter of concern to the AFAG, since it remained high compared to USAF standards. There were 18 aircraft mishaps in January, ten of which were due to pilot error, and 25 accidents in April. In June, the VNAF experienced 19 aircraft mishaps-- four were lost to combat; four were major aircraft accidents; five were minor aircraft accidents; and six were reported incidents. These mishaps accounted for four fatalities, with a total of seven aircraft lost during June. There were 23 mishaps during July, resulting in 24 fatalities, five planes lost, seven major accidents, and six reportable incidents. Twelve accidents were due to pilot error, two were due to material failure, one to faulty supervision, one to poor maintenance, and three to combat. Considering the increase in hours and sorties flown during the year, however, the accident rate showed a healthy downward trend. In this area, a stringent and continuing safety education program was being waged at all levels of command.[32/]

One of the most recognizable general achievements of the VNAF was its sustained and effective support of the ARVN in accomplishing its mission in all four Corps areas, especially the IV Corps location. It was felt that VNAF was accomplishing its mission more effectively due in a large measure to improvements in command and control, individual and unit morale, application of better managerial practice and procedures, advances in night support for attack and helicopter aircraft, and general VNAF convergence to a condition of maturity and stabilization.[33/]

VNAF operations were affected to some degree by dissident political turmoil in Da Nang during May. The 522d Fighter Squadron was deployed from Tan Son Nhut to Da Nang, where it flew 91 sorties on airborne alert. The 516th Fighter Squadron, stationed at Da Nang, canceled BLACK EYE strike operations over NVN indefinitely on 14 May, due to the I CTZ local situation and flew many airborne alert missions instead. VNAF fighter operations in II, III and IV CTZs were hampered only to a minor degree, as some fighters were deployed from these areas to Da Nang. VNAF transport operations were heavily affected, however, as airlift squadrons flew 133 percent of their programmed flying hours.[34/]

VNAF participation in visual armed reconnaissance in the ROLLING THUNDER program, Operation BLACK EYE, was suspended as a daily program in July, after a total of 483 sorties, of which 243 were flown in that month.

Future VNAF participation in ROLLING THUNDER was to be limited to occasional armed reconnaissance flights. Actually, VNAF did not fly any additional out-of-country sorties during the remainder of the year and concentrated instead on direct support of ARVN in South Vietnam. 35/

The departing Chief, AFAG, made the following comments about VNAF in October 1966: 36/

> "...The Vietnamese Air Force today is a healthy child that needs to mature. He suffers from growing pains and many problems remain to be solved. However, we are aware of the problems and the progress made by VNAF during my tour in Vietnam convinces me that they have the potential and are well on the way to becoming one of the most efficient and effective Air Forces in the Far East. The money, time, and effort we have spent have been a wise investment...."

Base Construction

The USAF and other armed services faced unique logistical problems in SEA. The limitations of South Vietnam's railroad network, security problems, and the character of military operations, made air mobility mandatory; this mobility required a rapidly expanding network of airfields. Accordingly, the construction of new airfields, and the maintenance and upgrading of existing facilities, received heavy emphasis during the year. 37/

MACV, USARV, and 7AF joined efforts to develop a master plan for upgrading airfields to insure availability of adequate air logistic support for tactical operations. The coordinating group decided that the primary requirement was for C-130 airfields, and that an all-weather capability of

60 C-130 sorties per a ten-hour day was required. It prepared a priority list of 40 airfields requiring upgrading to C-130 capability, which received COMUSMACV approval in June, and was later expanded to 62 facilities. The shortage of materiel, however, particularly airfield matting, and the changing military situation, impeded progress. By the end of the year, An Hoa, Duc Pho, Quang Ngai, Dong Ha, and Khe Sanh had acquired C-130 capability. Although much remained to be done, by March 1967, South Vietnam had 88 airfields with C-130 capability; 32 were classified as Type I-minimum operational; 41 as Type II-marginal operational; and 15 were Type III-fully operational. It had 130 C-123 airfields: Type I-36; Type II-77; Type III-17. The 155 C-7A airfields were as follows: Type I-41; Type II-95; Type III-19. By early 1967, there were also 8 airfields with 14 jet-capable runways (Tan Son Nhut-2; Bien Hoa-2; Cam Ranh Bay-2; Phan Rang-2; Chu Lai-2; Da Nang-2; Phu Cat-1; and Tuy Hoa-1). 38/

Airfield maintenance presented another serious problem. U.S. fixed-wing aircraft were using, in varying degrees, more than 200 airfields in South Vietnam. Shortages of construction material and the limited number of available engineer troops greatly complicated the maintenance of such a large number of airfields during a combat situation. 39/

MCP Funding Problems

Limited by insufficient funds and because contract costs were rapidly being escalated, the entire Military Construction Program (MCP) was readjusted at a CINCPAC conference in April 1966. By June, however, the program was still in jeopardy, because of accelerating costs. The situation was reviewed with the Navy Officer in Charge of Construction (OICC), and it was determined that overall, 7AF needed some 80 million dollars to complete approved programs. This same situation was true for the other services, and the matter was referred to the Office of the Secretary of Defense. The final decision was to apportion a part of the deficit in November 1966, with a promise to pay the balance on 1 April 1967. Accordingly, 17.4 million dollars was finally made available in December 1966, and construction directives were issued by MACV to cover these items. 40/

The MCP was underfunded to the extent of 63 million dollars by the end of the year. The OICC consented, however, to spread the remaining dollars on the basis of starting items, where it was clear that the total funds for a project would not be spent by April. This action promised to permit notices to proceed on an additional 15 to 20 million dollars more than the 17.4 percent previously funded. The impact on 7AF of this cost-overrun was quite serious, since many items in the program would be constructed as much as one year late.

Cam Ranh Bay and Phan Rang were only partially completed at the end of the year and Phu Cat AB had to rely on a single Red Horse Squadron (Civil Engineering Heavy Repair Squadrons) for almost all of its vertical construction support. Bases would have to continue to operate with inadequate facilities in many instances as a result of construction slippage. The situation was expected to improve in 1967, however, when much of the construction would be completed. 41/

Project Turnkey

The signing of the Turnkey contract on 31 May 1966, represented a major breakthrough for the Air Force. It was the first time the Air Force's construction of an entire base had been permitted without recourse to the Army or Navy. Furthermore, the Turnkey concept provided construction for an entire base as opposed to a series of line items, which might frequently fail to materialize in their entirety. Project Turnkey was operated through the Director of Civil Engineering, 7AF who was designated Program Director. 42/

Tuy Hoa AB

The construction of an air base at Tuy Hoa, under the Turnkey concept, was to become a highly controversial project. There was considerable discussion initially as to the site location. During a CINCPAC conference in January, the PACOM staff expressed increasing doubt as to the feasibility of Tuy Hoa. They pointed out that the artificial harbor for this area could not be finished before the end of 1966. Because of this, the airfield would be inoperative during the monsoon season, unless it was supplied by air, which was considered impractical. Qui Nhon was favored because of its location at the terminus of Route 19, the existence of a port, and the presence of security forces in the area. 43/

CINCPAC questioned the construction at Tuy Hoa, without regard to logistic difficulty. He told JCS that he concurred with COMUSMACV that saturation of airfields was a major concern and that the problem was particularly acute at Da Nang. He did not believe, however, that relocating

75

units from Da Nang to Tuy Hoa, would be the answer from an operational point of view. He felt that the best way to relieve congestion and improve operational capability, was to construct an additional airfield in the Da Nang, Hue/Phu Bai area. He assumed that the key problem at Hue/Phu Bai was the difficulty in obtaining real estate and construction, under the political situation at that time. Unless there were permanent overriding political considerations, however, he believed that the Hue/Phu Bai area was still the best choice. 44/

COMUSMACV pointed out in April that Tuy Hoa seemed to be the only solution in the near-time frame. Although the Hue/Phu Bai location was preferred, he pointed out that the political situation was so disturbing that it would be impossible to start construction there in time to have the project finished before the northeast monsoon began. 45/

Mobilization at Tuy Hoa started in July, with major ship unloading commencing in August. The initial phase of Turnkey provided an AM2 runway, taxiway, and apron complex supported by certain buildings in December 1966. This goal was realized, and the base actually accommodated an operational squadron on 15 November, 45 days ahead of schedule. This squadron was followed by a second on 9 December, and a third on 16 December, which placed a full wing in operation. By 31 December 1966, approximately 2,950 personnel were in place at Tuy Hoa. The status at the end of the year indicated that the sustained operational facility could be completed by the scheduled date of 31 May 1967. 46/

Sentry Dog and Handler in Southeast Asia
Figure 2

Cam Ranh Bay AB

At the start of 1966, Cam Ranh Bay AB was supporting the 12th Tactical Fighter Wing from a 10,000-foot AM2 runway, taxiway, and apron system. Personnel were housed in tents; facilities, roads, and utilities were virtually nonexistent. Construction was scheduled to start in January, on a permanent PCC airfield system, and a series of sustained operational facilities, such as buildings, roads, and utilities. Due to severe shipping and storage problems in association with the Cam Ranh Bay Port and Army Depot, MACV decided to remove all contractor effort on the base for six months. Construction of sustained operational facilities thus came to a virtual standstill until June 1966, at which time work was resumed on the air base.[47/]

By October, 8,000 feet of the 10,000-foot PCC runway were completed and placed in operation. A parallel concrete taxiway followed in November. A 90,000-yard AM2 apron was constructed concurrently, with the runway providing for operation of heavy aircraft. As a result, the Military Airlift Command commenced operation at the base in November. At the end of the year, approximately 6,000 personnel lived in tent-type facilities on the fighter side of the base. The entire airfield complex with sufficient sustaining operational facilities on both sides of the base to support essential elements of each mission, should be completed in 1967.[48/]

Phu Cat AB

Due to limited funding and cost-overrun problems, COMUSMACV directed that only the airfield complex, base roads, utilities, POL, ammunition area, and control tower be provided through contractual action under the OICC. Vertical construction, except for items mentioned previously, was tasked to 7AF to be accomplished by the 819th Civil Engineering Heavy Repair Squadron. The contractor's base camp was erected by Korean subcontractors commencing in May, and work on the airfield progressed satisfactorily, until the monsoons occurred in late fall, when production came to a virtual standstill. The 819th CES, which arrived on base in September, succeeded in completing nine dormitories and installing a temporary AM2 apron adjacent to a 3,000-foot dirt strip. The base was scheduled for an operational date in April, for fighter-type aircraft; however, in November, it was decided to put two C-7A squadrons in operation at Phu Cat on 1 January 1967. Work schedules for the contractor and the 819th CES were adjusted to meet this objective. 49/

Phan Rang AB

The interim AM2 airfield layout was under construction at the start of 1966. On 15 March, the first squadron and elements of the 366th Wing Headquarters commenced operation from the base. Operation was started from a 10,000-foot AM2 runway, a partially completed taxiway system, and a portion of apron sufficient to handle the one unit. Five squadrons were in operation by midsummer. The AM2 airfield system, however, started to fail rapidly in May, with the advent of unseasonable rains. The efforts of the 554th Heavy Repair Squadron were devoted almost exclusively to keeping the airfield in operation, until the new concrete runway was opened in October.

Munitions areas, the road system, dormitories, and other facilities were started during the year, but due to cost overruns much of the originally-planned vertical construction was held in abeyance. It was anticipated that by 1967, Phan Rang would be a complete facility. 50/

The Secretary of the Air Force said in February 1966, that we had "learned some valuable lessons which should accelerate site selection and construction in the future." He pointed out that it was important to identify potential base sites in a theater early, and in adequate numbers to meet foreseeable operational requirements and avoid costly delays in site selections.

The Secretary of the Air Force stated further that heavy repair squadrons were needed as a permanent part of the Air Force's tactical force, not only to provide an organic repair and base maintenance capability but also a limited construction capability. Stockpiles of construction and base maintenance equipment, materials, and packaged facilities would enable the U.S. to support combat operations rapidly. He noted that where a contractor could be used instead of engineer construction troops, the Turnkey concept developed by the Air Force appeared to offer a good way of providing new construction rapidly with the least impact on in-country construction capacity, logistic support facilities, and inflation of the local economy. 51/

Base Defense

The focus of attention was on base defense at an increasing number of bases and this remained a critical problem throughout the year. At a relatively small cost in casualties, the Viet Cong were able to mount numerous successful attacks against airfields during the year which resulted in U.S. and South Vietnamese personnel losses and material damage to aircraft and other material.

The first attack of 1966 (Appendix I) occurred on 25 January when 20 81-mm mortar rounds landed near the billeting area at Da Nang AB, and the year ended with a second attack against Tan Son Nhut. [52] The attacks revealed a recurring pattern in which some or all of the following conditions were observed: [53]

- Normally were preceded by a period of 15-30 days, during which increased enemy activity was noted in areas near the base. This activity took the form of increased terrorism in villages and hamlets, attacks on RP/PF and ARVN outposts, mining of roads, ambushes, and in some cases, actually probes on base perimeters. A higher-than-normal absenteeism rate among local nationals was also noted at one base on the night the attack occurred.

- Lasted 20 minutes or less, with the majority in the range of 10-15 minutes.

- Showed thorough, detailed planning and a comprehensive knowledge of troop and materiel dispositions within the base. The enemy also took advantage of fixed patterns of activity.

- Normally were carried out during periods of lowered visibility, either during overcast weather conditions or nights without moonlight.

- Aircraft parking ramps, both fixed and rotary wing, were major targets.

- Countermortar radar capability was generally inadequate to provide positive locations of enemy weapons positions so that effective counterfire action could be taken.

From these conditions, certain lessons and conclusions were reached: [54]

* During periods of increased enemy activity in areas adjacent to bases, effective communication and coordination among USAF security forces, the Administrative Coordinator, external US/FWMAF and MACV advisory detachments and Popular and ARVN forces were essential. This permitted effective procedures and working relationships to be developed prior to any emergency which might develop. Coordination and cooperation among these agencies contributed to early recognition and dissemination of attack indicators, development of effective procedures and working relationships before an attack, and more rapid reaction and smoother operations during an attack.

* In the past, attacks on bases had consisted of standoff mortar/recoilless rifle fire, the so-called "suicide/commando" raid, or a combination of both. The rapidity with which the attacks were executed called for consideration of several areas. [55]

    1. An adequate security force must be in position to detect, give early warning, and blunt initial effectiveness of any attack.

    2. Ground alert aircraft had become airborne and delivered fire on enemy weapons before cessation of an attack, but a five-minute scramble time gave the enemy an interval for numerous rounds on the target. Avoiding this potential loss, justified in some measure the maintenance of an airborne firepower capability over the base during prime attack hours.

    3. Methods and procedures for coordination of firepower support, to include authority to fire or otherwise engage hostile forces by airborne aircraft, security forces, and defending ground forces when the base was under actual attack, were complicated by split jurisdiction over areas within and adjacent to certain air bases. This matter had to be resolved if the full weight of the defense was to be employed rapidly and decisively.

    4. Insufficient primary and backup communications capability, together with inadequate communications discipline, hampered the flow of intelligence, orders, and other vital traffic during emergencies. Action had to be taken to insure adequate primary and secondary

communications among all agencies involved in base defense, and to provide two noninterfering radio channels to USAF Air Police squadrons exclusively for security use.

* Since the enemy invariably exploited inflexible or stereotyped actions, certain measures could be implemented to disrupt enemy planning and execution and reduce effectiveness of his attacks, for example: 56/

    1. Random scheduling of aerial firepower cover during "prime" attack periods.

    2. Random illumination of areas adjacent to the base, using aerial flareships.

    3. Revetting of aircraft parking areas.

    4. Maximum dispersal of unrevetted aircraft.

    5. Placing green alert aircraft and crews at random locations on the base, away from normal parking areas, with locations varied frequently.

    6. Varying placement of sentries, including K-9, on the perimeter and in critical areas.

    7. Random use of vehicular patrols throughout the base and the perimeter.

    8. Frequent patrol and ambush activities by external forces adjacent to the base, particularly during "prime" attack periods.

    9. Improved entry and exit screening of local national laborers and other employees to eliminate, insofar as possible, infiltration of enemy agents or sympathizers onto the base.

* A high order of reliance could not be placed on effectiveness of one countermortar radar, AN/MPQ 4A, for all bases. Action was initiated to secure a minimum of one radar for all bases, with additional sets as required for selected bases. COMUS-MACV also took action to secure a new type of 360-degree countermortar radar for numerous facilities throughout the country, including all jet-capable bases. 57/

MORTAR ATTACK at Tan Son Nhut- April 66
Figure 3

Logistics

The rapid logistic buildup in 1966 brought problems of aircraft maintenance, supply and services, munitions, etc. In his End of Tour Report, the Deputy Commander, 7AF, stated: 58/

> "...To date, the overall logistic support has been barely adequate. In fact, it has been marginal on many occasions. Our success has been due mostly to the top priority assigned for SEA, outstanding and dedicated work by thousands of people in the ZI, and the perseverance of the airmen in SEA. In reviewing the reasons for non-operational aircraft, the nouns were all too familiar. They were the same parts that had been proved to be required in the past, and the same parts that were required in quantity in War Readiness Materiel (WRM) kits. After logistics requirements are determined from good operational experience, I believe that we must take a stronger position in obtaining and maintaining WRM. It must be completely over and above operating requirements and the pipeline necessary to support this segment. Furthermore the quantity must be sufficient to support the combat flying hour program under the maintenance conditions that we know will exist...."

Ordnance

One of the most controversial problems of 1966, pertained to munitions shortages and their effect upon combat operations. At the beginning of the year, the following air munitions were reportedly in short supply: the 40-mm grenade for launch from helicopters, the air-delivered 2.75-inch rockets, 20-mm HE cannon ammunition, the MK-81 250-pound bomb, the MK-82 500-pound bomb, and the M-117 750-pound bomb. 59/

At a USAF munitions allocation conference held in Washington, during 11-12 January 1966, it was determined that available munitions would support

400 ARC LIGHT sorties per month through March, 450 through June, and 600 for the last six months of the year. Conferees also estimated that approximately 3,000 STEEL TIGER, BARREL ROLL, and TIGER HOUND sorties could be mounted each month. Available munitions would permit an average load of 1.7 tons per sortie (2.1 in NVN and 1.55 in SVN/Laos).

The conference allocated USAF munitions for the first quarter of CY 1966, and projected allocations for the balance of the year. MACV J-4 stated that "although allocations to PACAF and VNAF fell short of requirements, projection is being increased sufficiently to meet estimated future requirements of all munitions except 2.75-inch rocket motors." Ammunition problems continued to develop, however, and by the end of April, the list of air munitions officially listed as critical had expanded to 13. With the exception of napalm, every other air munition at some time and to some degree was in short supply. 60/

In a briefing in Saigon on 3 April, Deputy Secretary of Defense, Cyrus R. Vance, was informed that the munitions shortage was critical and that production would not meet requirements before 1967. Headquarters USAF had been forced to allocate them to its major commands on the basis of existing inventories and production, and as a result, bomb loads were being reduced and substitute munitions were being used.

The Secretary of Defense was advised that only 73 percent of the required bomb assets, and only 33 percent of the required CBU-2 assets, were available. The 7AF reported that 44 ROLLING THUNDER, 32 STEEL TIGER, and 4 BARREL ROLL missions had been canceled because of the shortage during the first ten days of April. No in-country missions had been canceled, but aircraft had been held on ground alert and 320 missions that normally would have been preplanned were not flown. From 11 to 14 April, 515 in-country airstrikes, that otherwise would have been flown, were not scheduled due to ordnance shortages. COMUSMACV considered the air munitions shortages an emergency situation seriously affecting airstrike capability in SEA, and he informed CINCPAC and JCS, accordingly, on 8 April. 61/

COMUSMACV developed the following system of priorities for management of in-country airstrikes by USAF:

> A--Support of units in contact
> B--Support of major operations
> C--Escort of convoys and trains
> D1--Targets directly affecting the ground situation
> D2--Lucrative, perishable targets
> D3--Lucrative, static targets.

To conserve munitions, only requests for strikes against categories through priority D1 were to be honored. Other steps taken to alleviate the shortage were the transfer of munitions among service components, temporary incursions into reserve stocks, and authorizing COMUSMACV to call on Yankee Station carriers to strike essential targets, if necessary. These management measures temporarily helped to alleviate specific problems, but the basic problems of production and transport did not lend themselves to any quick, easy solution. 62/

At a conference held in Honolulu from 11-13 April to discuss the SEA munitions problem, these decisions were made: (1) to develop realistic sortie plans by month, weapon, and service; (2) to provide operating stock levels; (3) to increase WESTPAC stock by drawing on CONUS stocks; (4) to provide better management for production of bomb components; (5) to establish a realistic pipeline; and (6) to accelerate production. [63]

The following sortie allocation for USAF forces was drawn up at the conference:

Month	NVN	SVN	Laos
Apr	1,600	7,159	4,420
May	2,100	7,159	3,920
Jun	2,600	9,079	3,420
Jul	3,100	9,079	2,920
Aug	3,100	10,468	2,920
Sep	3,100	10,468	2,920
Oct	2,600	11,062	3,420
Nov	2,600	11,062	3,420
Dec	1,600	12,250	4,420
	22,400	87,786	31,780

Based on this allocation, the tonnage per sortie per month was not to exceed an average of 2.4 tons for NVN and 1.65 tons for SVN and Laos. This allowed 7AF to increase or decrease tonnage per sortie for in-country and out-country strikes at the command's discretion. The overall objective was to attain the maximum feasible number of sorties consistent with effective munition loadings and with the required tonnage limitations. When it became evident that lucrative fleeting targets had to be struck in violation of these guidelines, the 7AF was advised by PACAF to provide notification of the target description, justification and relative importance of the target, and the estimated amounts of munitions which would be in excess of authorized amounts. [64]

PACAF also informed 7AF that extraordinary efforts were made to deploy available munitions to SEA, and that the physical availability of these assets should in no way influence the command to expend munitions in excess of those limits set by CINCPAC. The 7AF's objective should be to achieve a 30-day on-base stockage at each SEA operating location. 65/

During the conference stories broke in the press concerning the shortages. The CJCS was concerned that some key congressmen apparently felt that the U.S. had overextended itself in SEA, and this obviously endangered continuation of the buildup. On 17 April 1966, the Deputy Secretary of Defense stated that "categorically there are no shortages which have adversely affected combat operations." He pointed out that in March, the U.S. dropped 50,000 tons of bombs, or three times the monthly average of the Korean War. He also quoted Chairman of the JCS, Gen. Earle G. Wheeler: "There have been no shortages in supplies for troops in SVN which have adversely affected combat operations or the health or welfare of our troops. No required air sorties have been canceled. As a matter of fact, the air support given our forces is without parallel in our history." The Deputy Secretary also stated that COMUSMACV told him the same thing as did all commanders with whom he had spoken while in SVN. 66/

COMUSMACV reviewed CINCPAC's evaluation of SEA air munitions availability and stated on 25 April 1966, that the U.S. would be in a position to maintain programmed sortie rates after substantially improving the supply of complete rounds. COMUSMACV believed careful planning was required to weaponeer strike forces, so that the weight of ordnance would be placed where it was most needed. It also required strict management controls and a constant reassessment of the tactical situation. To provide maximum flexibility in tactical operations called for the utmost efforts in replenishing stocks. 67/

In June, the Secretary of Defense questioned whether the Air Force could effectively consume, in planned operations, more than 60,000 tons of munitions per month. PACAF's reply touched on the overall philosophy of air operations in SEA. The reduction of munitions expenditure to 60,000 tons a month would result in about 1.6 tons average load for attack sorties based on planned sortie capabilities for 1967. According to PACAF, the use of lightly-loaded jet fighters for daytime armed reconnaissance would prove unrewarding. The use of "guns only" or "guns and rockets" munitions in heavily defended areas would require that strike fighters penetrate automatic and small arms lethal envelopes. Such penetrations would result in an increased loss rate without a commensurate increase in effectiveness.

In SEA, PACAF further responded that experience over the past year (June 65-June 66) had shown that strike fighters, loaded with optimum ordnance and scheduled against validated targets, were the most effective way of using the strike fighter force in NVN, Laos, and to a major extent, in South Vietnam. 68/

PACAF reported that in August, munitions deliveries had improved the situation materially and stocks on hand had increased substantially in terms of total tonnage. The desired types of weapons, however, were not available in all instances. This resulted in aircraft carrying less tonnage than would be possible if ordnance were possessed in the desired types and numbers. 69/

The shortage reached its peak by midyear when the overall stockage levels in 7AF had fallen to 15 days against a 45-day objective. Then the situation began to improve and by 15 August, the stockage levels had climbed to 30 days. This improvement, which continued for the remainder of the year, was due to increased production in CONUS and increased ammunition inventories in WESTPAC. 70/

In his End of Tour Report, the Deputy Commander, 7AF, made the following comments pertaining to the munitions problem: 71/

> "...Again, as in Korea, munitions problems have plagued the Command from the onset of our participation in the current conflict. These problems stem from a shortage of trained personnel and support equipment to handle the large tonnage associated with this activity. UMDs of Fighter Squadrons were woefully inadequate in authorizing the numbers of personnel required for storage, handling, loading and supplying our munitions activities. 'Top Dog' personnel were supplied on a TDY basis, after receiving only minimum training to meet initial shortages. Unfortunately, about the time they really became knowledgeable and productive, their TDY period expired and they were replaced with other TDY people. Sufficient time has now elapsed to permit all PCS assignment of the required people to accomplish this function. The important lesson to be learned again is that munitions personnel are a 'must' and have to be retained in our fighter forces during peacetime periods if we want the capability to fight the force on an immediate basis...."

CHAPTER V

FRIENDLY AIR OPERATIONS

Introduction

There were several separate conflicts or wars in SEA in which the Air Force played a significant role. There was the so-called "in-country" war in South Vietnam and two somewhat separate conflicts in Laos. The one in northern Laos was designed to counter aggression itself, while the one in the South was aimed primarily at cutting the supply lines between North Vietnam and South Vietnam that went through Laos. Air action in North Vietnam continued during the year in an effort to force curtailment of Hanoi's support of the conflict in SEA. 1/

Interdiction - Aerial

The effort to stem the flow of men and material from North Vietnam into South Vietnam resulted in a proliferation of interdiction programs under various code names. Among the major programs was BARREL ROLL, initiated on 24 December 1964, which had the mission of interdicting the North Vietnamese supply lines that fell within northern Laos, as well as providing close air support of the Force Armee Royale (FAR) and Meo soldiers. 2/

The BARREL ROLL program continued during 1966, with strikes against personnel and equipment coming from North Vietnam in support of the Pathet Lao and Viet Minh forces. Both RVN and Thai-based U.S. aircraft were used for the BARREL ROLL program, and the latter were employed for close air

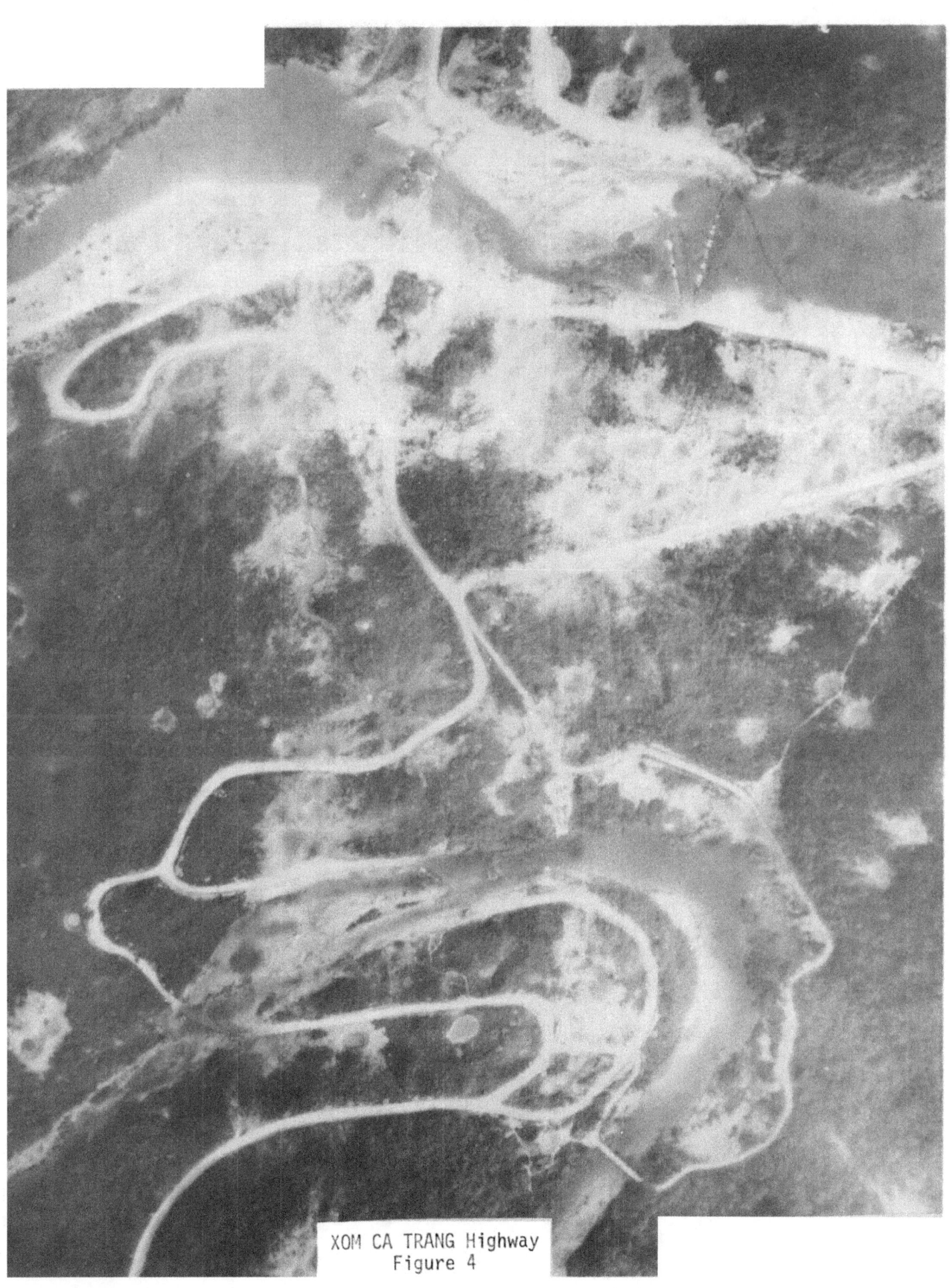

XOM CA TRANG Highway
Figure 4

support in specified areas. The objective of this program was to destroy
enemy troop concentrations, and storage and supply complexes, thereby
reducing the enemy's capability to attack friendly-held territories in
northern Laos. The F-4C and F-105 strike aircraft, under the direction of
the A-1E forward air controllers, were employed for this program. The
supply areas and troop concentration targets were selected from the USAIRA,
Vientiane, recommended priority list of the RLAF. In addition, the all-
source intelligence reports were used to uncover and generate other targets
for the program, including day and night visual and armed reconnaissance of
major LOCs.

Major strike efforts included concentration on such lucrative storage
and supply complexes, as the Sam Neua, Ban Ban, and Nong Het supply depots
located along Routes 6, 7 and 65. Fleeting targets, such as vehicles and
troops, also were struck by visual and armed reconnaissance along the
major routes in the BARREL ROLL area. As a result of the day and night
sorties, buildings were destroyed and damaged and numerous secondary explosions were seen. One lesson learned from the BARREL ROLL program was
that the increased familiarity of the FACs with the area, and their ability
to accurately mark targets increased the effectiveness of the strike aircraft. This resulted in a substantial loss of the enemy and material during
1966. [3/]

STEEL TIGER

BARREL ROLL was divided into two programs in April 1965, to insure
that the interdiction efforts in the northern and southern BARREL ROLL areas

received equal emphasis. The second program was named STEEL TIGER and covered that portion of eastern Laos, south of the 17th parallel. 4/

The STEEL TIGER program continued during 1966 to harass and impede the flow of men and material into South Vietnam. The program remained one of maintaining visual and armed reconnaissance over key LOCs and selected interdiction points. Strikes were directed by O-1 and AC-47 forward air controllers. Primary targets were selected through the use of the all-source intelligence information, which included Road Watch, CAS, FAC/VR, and other reports. When FAC control was not available, alternate targets were provided. These consisted of fixed RLAF targets and selected interdiction points. Considerable effort was expended along Route 23, south of the Mu Gia Pass, to the junction of Route 911. From that point, emphasis was placed south on Route 911 to the junction of Route 91 and to Route 912, which connected Routes 137 (NVN) and Route 911 (Laos).

Strikes were also carried out at selected route interdiction points, so as to impede the flow of materiel through backlogging traffic along these routes. During the year, the enemy activity was impeded and harassed as a result of the STEEL TIGER program. His activity was hampered because of the capability of the FAC and strike aircraft to respond quickly to a developing situation as indicated by current intelligence. 5/

TIGER HOUND

Since the STEEL TIGER operation had not achieved full effectiveness in containing the infiltration of men and material into South Vietnam, it had been divided into two parts in December 1965, resulting in Project TIGER HOUND. 6/

From the beginning of TIGER HOUND operations in December 1965, results slowly increased in January 1966, began a sharp rise in February and March, which peaked in April, and then started a sharp decline in May. Infiltration had not ceased, but conditions had forced a change in enemy methods. With continued interdiction of LOCs, and the heavy monsoon rains, the roads were impassable. At the end of June, bomb craters, mud slides, and swollen rivers closed all motorable roads, except for short stretches. Intelligence confirmed that a new supply route through the DMZ was developed for the purpose of sustaining newly-infiltrated/NVN units operating in Quang Tri Province, South Vietnam.

To counter the enemy's shift in operational area, TALLY HO was begun in July, utilizing the experience gained in TIGER HOUND. The reallocation of resources in July, with TIGER HOUND/TALLY HO reduced TIGER HOUND operating bases from five to three. Activity and results in the TIGER HOUND area continued to decrease during July, and as a result only 2,190 TIGER HOUND sorties were flown that month as compared to 3,560 in June.

In August, monsoon rains forced a large number of sorties to be expended under Combat Skyspot control. The main emphasis in the strikes was to keep roads interdicted, to hit suspected truck parks, storage areas, and small troop concentrations.

During September, the enemy appeared to be relying more and more on river boats to transport supplies. Indications were that the change to boats was necessary, since the motorable roads remained impassable and supplies were needed by enemy forces to the east. It was nearly impossible, however, to ascertain that the boats were actually transporting military supplies and, therefore, under the Rules of Engagement, it was impossible to strike them.

In addition, difficulties had been experienced in striking the augmented bicycle traffic of the trails. Despite increased enemy activity on the trails and rivers in TIGER HOUND, LOC status at the end of September on the motorable roads remained unchanged. With improvement of the weather in October, FACs observed signs of increasing road repair. Enemy forces continued to increase during the month as evidenced by strike results and ground fire reports. Operations throughout November were largely hampered by weather in the TIGER HOUND area and at the strike aircraft bases. 7/

Although the first six months of TIGER HOUND operations were the most productive, the total results as of 31 December 1966, were as follows: 8/

Trucks Dest/Damg	Road Cuts, Cratered or Seeded	Landslides	Structures Damg/Dest
938/576	1,850	184	1,388/4,120

Enemy KBA	Watercraft Dest/Damg	AAA/AW Psns Dest/Damg	Secondary Explosions
403	33/16	125/70	1,717

Operation TALLY HO

During 1966, TIGER HOUND assets and procedures were used to stem infiltration through the DMZ. This operation known as TALLY HO was initiated on 17 July 1966. It was conceived in response to intelligence, which firmly established that the 324th B Division of the NVN Army had crossed the DMZ, and had massed in Quang Tri Province. As TIGER HOUND operations were being thinned out, concurrent with the inception of TALLY HO operations, it was decided that the TIGER HOUND staff would manage TALLY HO. COMUSMACV made it clear, however, that TIGER HOUND was not to be abandoned. He estimated that TALLY HO would probably continue into January 1967, when it was likely that emphasis would shift back into the TIGER HOUND area. 9/

TIGER HOUND procedures were to be used in the TALLY HO area to achieve maximum interdiction of enemy forces immediately south of the DMZ, immediately north of the DMZ, and along the Laos border into the Lao Bao area. The concept of operations for TALLY HO was based on visual reconnaissance performed principally by airborne FACs flying in pairs in O-1Es and escorted by A-1Es. The basic concept in O-1E utilization was to keep these aircraft working within a permissive environment, but all FACs agreed that the TALLY HO area was the most heavily defended location in which they had flown.

As a result, the limits of a safe operation area for the O-1Es was identified, and directions were issued to the FACs not to penetrate beyond this line of limitations. FACs were initially excluded from night operations, but, it became apparent that, while many lucrative targets were being spotted and struck during daylight hours, most of the fleeting targets were to be found at night. After some experimentation with night operations, the O-1Es were allowed in August, to go back into the TALLY HO area at night. They were fragged on strictly visual reconnaissance (VR) missions and had no authority to call in strikes on targets. 10/

Beginning late in July, the VNAF conducted a number of strikes in the western part of the TALLY HO sector known as the BLACK EYE area. The Commander, 7AF, however, directed that they be withdrawn as the VNAF strikes were not controlled by TALLY HO FACs. Coordination and control requirements dictated that VNAF not operate in the area. 11/

There was general concern in September that the 324th B Division was preparing for a major offensive. To counter this threat, Operation GRAND SLAM--a 36-hour concentrated air attack centered around two target areas in the DMZ--was implemented on 16 September. The lack of suitable targets, however, plus deteriorating weather, prevented an official declaration of GRAND SLAM. The major enemy offensive did not take place at that time, but it was believed by some that the threat still existed. 12/

An effort to honor and restore the DMZ, according to provisions of the 1954 Geneva Convention, resulted in a temporary cessation of military operations in the eastern portion of that area on 26 September. There were numerous violations by the enemy, however, and the trial suspension ended on 13 October. 13/

The monsoon, which started in October, turned the upper half of the

TALLY HO area into a lake, and there were indications that boats were being used to transit the flooded roads, after which the enemy offloaded to the trucks. A curfew was placed on all rivers, coastal waters, and canals within Quang Tri Province on 20 October. Possible SAMs in the TALLY HO area were also detected at this time. [14]

Although Operation TALLY HO did not stop the flow of men and material, it considerably altered the enemy's pattern of infiltration. He was no longer free to move at will and more of his time was being spent in road repair, camouflage and dispersal of supplies. From the beginning of TALLY HO on 20 July, through 30 November, accumulative statistics revealed the following: [15]

Trucks Dest/Damg	Road Cuts, Cratered or Seeded	Landslides	Structures Dest/Damg
72/61	339	6	1,208/624
Enemy KBA	Watercraft Dest/Damg	AAA/AAW Psns Dest/Damg	Secondary Explosions
135	85/132	91/22	1,414

ARC LIGHT Program

In addition to its other missions, the ARC LIGHT program also included providing assistance in the interdiction effort. One of the most dramatic and highly publicized interdiction efforts undertaken during 1966 was the B-52 bombing of Mu Gia Pass. At a conference held at Udorn on 8 March 1966, attended by COMUSMACV and the Ambassadors to Thailand and Laos, it was agreed that the majority of truck traffic infiltrating into South Vietnam was coming through this pass. It had been interdicted over the past several months but with limited success. Studies had revealed a vulnerable segment of the road, however, which it was believed could be cut by use of a saturation bombing technique. Since the tactical bombing effort was degraded during the rainy season, COMUSMACV stated this would be the appropriate time to hit the choke point with B-52 strikes.[16/]

Shortly after the conference, the Commander, 7AF, in a target recommendation accepted by COMUSMACV, requested B-52 strikes on a vulnerable road segment in the Mu Gia Pass located approximately five nautical miles south of the NVN border in Laos. The targeted area would encompass intersection of highway Routes 12 and 23, including one bridge crossing a narrow canyon between two ridge lines, where bypassing would be very difficult.

Tactical forces had cut roads daily in this area, but repairs and bypasses were usually accomplished within a few hours, due to the small number of bombs delivered per strike. The B-52 bomb loads delivered in the rainy season would, in addition to bridge and road destruction, result in landslide coverage and make repairs more difficult. Bomb fuzing could be set for maximum cratering with added repair harassment by variable delayed fuzes when available. COMUSMACV recommended repeated strikes at irregular intervals by small forces of B-52s to maintain interdiction.[17/]

On 9 April, CINCPAC authorized execution of a B-52 strike, Rock Kick III (Quang Tri 15), which was carried out on 12 April. It was the first use of the massive B-52 bombardment pattern for road interdiction. Success in closing the pass by these strikes was only temporary, as the road was reopened to limited traffic only 24 hours after the Rock Kick III strike. Visual sightings and night surveillance photography indicated that the Mu Gia Pass was soon supporting extensive road traffic.[18]

Accordingly, it was struck again on 27 April 1966, but closure was effective for only 18 hours, since thousands of laborers made interim repairs. The Secretary of State on 26 April, said that the Mu Gia Pass experience had cast some doubts on the ability of the B-52 aircraft to accomplish landslides by area bombing.[19]

On 27 April, the 7AF informed the National Military Command Center (NMCC) and CINCPAC that one of its tactical aircraft had been hit by a missile in the Mu Gia area, thereby posing a threat to the B-52s.[20]

On 30 April, CINCPAC recommended to JCS against further use of ARC LIGHT forces in closing the Mu Gia Pass. From his assessment of the enemy's SA-2 missile potential in the area, and in consideration of the degree of effectiveness which could be expected in closing the pass, he concluded that B-52 employment in this case was not the best use of limited munitions assets. The objective of the ARC LIGHT program was to seek, find, and destroy war-making materials (rather than to concentrate on route blockage), which should continue to be the primary effort. Such effort could be seriously diluted by extensive support required for ARC LIGHT strikes in the Mu Gia area, with no assurance that COMUSMACV's blockage concept would achieve desired results.[21]

ROLLING THUNDER

Air operations against North Vietnam--ROLLING THUNDER--also had the objective of interdicting the flow of men and materiel into the South. All facets of the ROLLING THUNDER program were greatly intensified and expanded in scope during 1966. The year began with Defense Secretary, Robert S. McNamara, defending this controversial program before the Senate Armed Services Committee. At the end of 1966, the air campaign was still the subject of heated debate, both at home and abroad. [22/]

The overall objective of the air campaign remained the same: to reduce to the maximum extent feasible North Vietnam's capability to support and direct the insurgency in SEA. To achieve this end, it was considered necessary to:

- Reduce/restrict North Vietnam's assistance from external sources;

- Destroy in depth those resources already in North Vietnam that contributed most to the support of aggression; destroy or deny use of all known permanent military facilities; and harass and disrupt military operations;

- Harass, disrupt, and impede movement of men and materials through southern NVN into Laos and SVN.

The greatest impact on North Vietnam would be through reduction of support from external sources and destruction of in-country high-value resources. Armed reconnaissance would be less productive, destruction-wise, but it was essential in keeping the lines of supply constantly disrupted and harassed to impede movement. [23/]

NVN RAILROAD BRIDGE cut by F-105 Thunderchief pilots
Figure 5

The U.S.-initiated peace offensive at the beginning of the year ended in failure. After a 37-day (24 December 1965-30 January 1966) bombing pause, which had been opposed by the JCS, the air campaign was resumed on a low key on 31 January. The bombing of Dien Bien Phu airfield on 6 February signaled the increasing tempo of air operations. The attack not only severely cratered and rendered the airfield unserviceable, but it had important psychological connotations. Hanoi regarded Dien Bien Phu as a symbol of French defeat in 1954, and its destruction undoubtedly had an adverse impact on North Vietnamese morale. [24/]

The effectiveness of ROLLING THUNDER operations continued to be hampered by political restrictions. Attacks were to be avoided over populated areas, and targets, such as hydropower plants; and locks and dams could be hit only when specifically designated by a CINCPAC directive. Strikes could be conducted no closer than 30 NM from the center of Hanoi; ten NM from the center of Haiphong; and a zone along the CHICOM border, 30 NM wide from the Laotian border east to 106 degrees and 25 NM wide from there to the Gulf of Tonkin. Flight paths to and from target areas had to be planned, so that they would not come any closer than 20 NM to the CHICOM border. Iron Hand missions, which had the objective of locating and destroying SAM sites, could be flown in conjunction with ROLLING THUNDER armed reconnaissance. The area of operations for Blue Tree photo reconnaissance would include all of North Vietnam, with the exception of restricted areas. [25/]

In a midyear assessment, CINCPAC concluded that North Vietnam was increasing its support of the war in South Vietnam. He noted that the air campaign against the North had made it more difficult for the enemy to infiltrate men and materials into South Vietnam, but it had not sufficiently reduced North Vietnam's capability to do so. The enemy had dispersed and concealed many of its high-value war-support resources, which made it difficult to find and destroy them. He had also built up stockpiles in North and South Vietnam, refined his support organization, and vastly increased his air defense. By the middle of 1966, the enemy had attained the capability of fielding and supporting more maneuver battalions in the South than had been previously estimated by CINCPAC. 26/

CINCPAC pointed out that only a limited portion of the concept for an effective air campaign promulgated in January 1966, had been carried out. This was armed reconnaissance in southern and northwestern North Vietnam and in Laos, along with very selective route interdiction in the northeast area. More than 99 percent of the operations conducted during the first six months were armed reconnaissance, concentrated primarily on dispersed enemy facilities and LOCs. The most important elements of the concept, however, had not been authorized. These were the denial of external assistance through closure of the major ports and heavy interdiction of LOCs leading from Communist China, coupled with in-depth destruction of those resources which supported aggression, particularly POL. 27/

North Vietnam's POL system was considered a most lucrative target from the standpoint of impairing the enemy's military logistics capability. The destruction of major POL storage areas would greatly complicate bulk offloading at ports and would necessitate new methods of offloading and transshipment, causing at least a temporary halt of POL to dispersed areas.

102

Since POL imports were not sufficient for the existing fleet of trucks, destruction of POL storage would further limit use of trucks and motorized watercraft.[28]

Approval to carry out the strikes against POL targets in the Hanoi/Haiphong areas was given only after the Secretary of Defense and the CJCS gave assurance to higher authority that every feasible step would be taken to minimize civilian casualties. In a coordinated operation on 29 June, the USAF struck the Hanoi petroleum storage area and the Navy struck the Haiphong petroleum storage area. Follow-up strikes against the Hanoi/Haiphong complex were made on 30 June and 1 July. It was estimated at the time that about two-thirds of North Vietnam's POL storage capability was destroyed in this three-day period. The strikes were viewed in some quarters as a serious escalation of the war and caused a domestic and international furor. The Secretary of Defense explained that the strikes against these petroleum facilities were initiated to counter a mounting reliance by North Vietnam on the use of trucks and powered junks to facilitate the infiltration of men and equipment from North Vietnam to South Vietnam.[29]

Plans were made and carried out to strangle the remaining POL supply by destroying POL installations, transitory targets, and the means by which POL was imported into North Vietnam. By the end of August, the USAF had destroyed 68 percent of the identified oil storage capacity authorized for attack in Route Packages 1, 5, and 6A. A new, dispersed storage capacity was being discovered, however, at a rate which approximated the rate of destruction.

The Air Force felt that POL attacks were becoming less productive as POL was being dispersed, but emphasis on these targets on a selective basis continued for the remainder of the year. CINCPAC recommended a "broadened target base designed to lead Hanoi to expect attacks anywhere, at any time, against any type of military target or activity that supports their aims." He believed that this broadened target base would be the most effective means of convincing Hanoi that the negotiating table was its best hope. 30/

Adverse weather conditions frequently made it impossible to maintain the desired level of interdiction against LOCs, particularly the northeast and northwest rail-lines. Although July and August were supposedly the months of best flying weather in North Vietnam, 81 percent of the sorties scheduled in Route Packages 5 and 6 were canceled or diverted because of weather. 31/

Although the enemy customarily took advantage of bombing pauses to resupply and reassign their troops, the year 1966 ended with a 48-hour truce over Christmas and the solar New Year. 32/

North Vietnam Defenses

During 1966, ROLLING THUNDER operations were conducted in an increasingly sophisticated defense environment. U.S. aircraft faced an effectively integrated system of radar-controlled antiaircraft weapons, surface-to-air

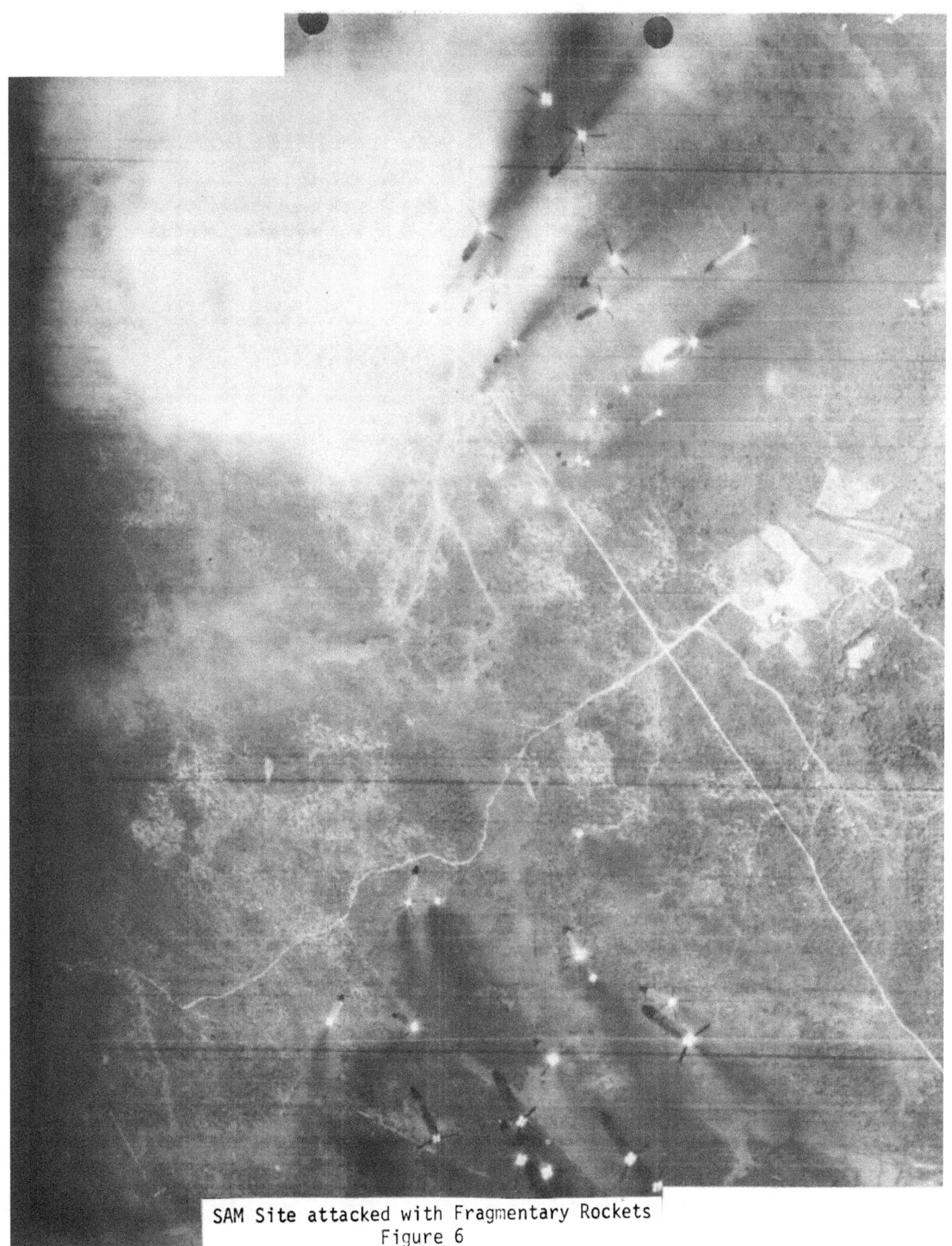

SAM Site attacked with Fragmentary Rockets
Figure 6

missiles and air intercept. These presented a continuing threat to the use of U.S. tactical airpower, particularly in areas well-known by the enemy to be sanctuaries. 33/

With the entire Red River Delta well-defended by the SA-2 system at the beginning of the year, Hanoi began to deploy firing battalions southward from Thanh Hoa. After the U.S. attacks against the Hanoi/Haiphong POL complex in June, most of the North Vietnamese SAM battalions south of Thanh Hoa were redeployed north into the Hanoi complex. The battalion structure in Hanoi thus became very compressed with firing units located five to seven miles apart. 34/

These heavily defended areas caused increasing aircraft losses and adversely affected strike tactics and results. Improved equipment and tactics did much to counter the threat, but nevertheless they were unable to overcome the main accomplishment of the missile; i.e., forcing aircraft to operate at lower altitudes where AAA and automatic weapons fire was more effective. 35/

CINCPAC stated that there was an urgent need for an improved Shrike missile that could find a target using a short emission and then lead the flight to it. Also needed were ample quantities of area weapons, such as CBU-24s, or other effective weapons to complete the destruction. This method of nullifying the threat, however, could never be completely successful, if villages or restricted areas were allowed to provide a sanctuary for sites or control centers. With regard to passive means of nullification, the ECM-B66s had not achieved the full degradation desired, but the

QRC 160-1 ECM POD was apparently highly effective.

If this effectiveness continued and the air fleet was completely equipped, nullification of the SA-2 threat, as well as the radar-controlled AAA, would have been enhanced. Since the enemy's most probable reaction would be continued and increased MIG defense, CINCPACAF suggested urgent use of ECM jamming of VHF communications as a method of negating the enemy's GCI control. [36]

During the first quarter of the year, the North Vietnamese Air Force continued previously established air tactics of committing fighters in combat, when the tactical advantage was clearly with the MIGs. But after 23 April, when U.S. aircraft first clashed with the new high-performance communist MIG-21s, the air war sharply intensified. By mid-August, the MIG aircraft were active almost every time strike forces penetrated to within 30 NM of Hanoi. Their tactics were no longer standard, and they could be expected to approach either from low level or from 15,000 to 20,000 feet. MIG activity reached a record high during December, when USAF aircraft had 35 encounters and 16 engagements involving 118 enemy aircraft. [37]

The increasing enemy air challenge again raised the question of bombing North Vietnamese jet-capable airfields, which the Commander, 7AF, had been advocating for some time. The Secretary of Defense had disapproved the strikes on the basis that military advantages did not outweigh military and political risks. In view of the new MIG aggressiveness, however, the CJCS asked CINCPAC to provide additional justification which he could present to the Secretary of Defense to secure approval to

GIA LAM AIRFIELD with parked
MIG 17 and MIG 21
Figure 7

bomb these airfields.[38]

In addition to the threat posed by MIG activity, the number of automatic weapons and antiaircraft artillery was believed to have increased from 5,000 to 7,400 during 1966. The majority of the newly-delivered guns were placed along the major LOCs and in the three major coastal city areas of Ron, Quang Khe, and Dong Hoi. The radar defense net also continued to show improved coordination among its various entities, so that by the end of the year, MIG activity, SAM launches, and AAA fire were noted as organized reactions against U.S. airstrikes.[39]

With Soviet and CHICOM technical and material assistance, North Vietnam by 1966 had established a complex defense system, which many military authorities described as the most formidable one ever faced by U.S. aircraft. The enemy's defensive environment was immeasurably aided by political sanctuaries and target restrictions, which limited the effectiveness of airpower.[40]

ROLLING THUNDER operations had succeeded, however, in destroying thousands of vehicles, including trucks, rolling stock, and watercraft. Movement of vital war material had been impeded by the destruction of hundreds of rail and highway bridges, and a large portion of the country's POL capability had also been destroyed. In addition, numerous structures, AAA, SAM, and radar sites had been destroyed or damaged. CINCPACAF noted at the end of the year that "without the disruption that was achieved by airpower, the Communist forces might long since have been able to marshal major forces for an all-out offensive towards South Vietnam." [41/]

The enemy had resorted to alternate means, however, of transporting war material, and had built bypasses and repaired bridges in minimum time. The attacks against the enemy's POL facilities had been offset by increased imports of POL and the rapid dispersal of the remaining POL stores. The enemy had also accomplished a major buildup of his air defense system, including a sophisticated EW/GCI network. [42/]

CINCPAC stated that the task of bringing the war to the doorstep of the North Vietnamese government had to be continued and intensified in 1967. He stressed that there should be no circles around Hanoi and Haiphong, denoting arbitrary areas of sanctuary. Instead, the target concept must be a simple one of attacking every significant military supply target. He felt that the exhaustion of men and material by the enemy could be done through attrition of war material, pressure on Hanoi, and aggressive search-and-destroy operations in South Vietnam. [43/]

INTERDICTION - GROUND

Barrier System

In addition to aerial interdiction, several other projects were initiated in an effort to halt the southward flow of men and materiel; i.e., the Barrier System, herbicide operations, and Project Popeye. On 17 September Defense Secretary McNamara tasked CINCPAC/MACV to "provide an infiltration interdiction system, to stop (or at a minimum to substantially reduce) the flow of men and supplies from north to South Vietnam." Joint Task Force

NORTH VIETNAMESE MIG is destroyed
Figure 8

728 was formed with the objective of having the system installed and in operation by 15 September 1967. The Director of the Joint Task Force was to report directly to the Secretary of Defense and was authorized direct contact with the JCS, the military services, and subordinate organizations. 44/

COMUSMACV stated on 21 September that the air-support portion of the proposed barrier could not be aided with resources that were being allocated to SVN, without seriously degrading the support of other operations. He noted that additional aircraft and air bases, such as Dong Ha, Khe Sanh, and Hue-Phu Bai, would require improvement to accommodate more aircraft. He stated that sorties of C-123 aircraft conducting herbicide operations, would have to be flown repeatedly to keep the area clear to dispense mines and acoustic detectors in the desired patterns. 45/

The installation of a strong point/early warning barrier system across South Vietnam, south of the DMZ, could be expected to result in increased infiltration and resupply efforts through Laos. It was believed that the enemy's efforts to skirt the ground barrier could be countered, and infiltration stopped or greatly reduced, by the selective use of Air Delivered Land Mines (ADLMs) and traffic sensor devices, in conjunction with an intensified interdiction program. The intensified interdiction operations plan was designed to form a moving, nonstatic system of air-delivered mine fields, traffic detection devices, and quick-reaction strike forces, which would impede and reduce enemy infiltration into South Vietnam. 46/

To support this plan, additional forces were to be programmed. It was envisioned that F-4 aircraft, utilized in the delivery of ADLMs, HE ordnance, and sensors, would be based at Hue/Phu Bai; C-130 aircraft, configured for sensor monitoring and ABCCC activities, would utilize Nakhon Phanom as a forward operating base; and Cam Ranh Bay would serve as their Main Operating Base (MOB). The O-2/OV-10 FAC aircraft (to be based at Nakhon Phanom), would be utilized in providing surveillance of the area, intelligence information, and direct airstrikes. The UC-123 aircraft would be used to provide defoliation support and would be based at Hue/Phu Bai, and CH-3 helicopters, to be located at Nakhon Phanom, would support special operations. 47/

The ground and air-delivered barriers formed only a part of the overall interdiction program--the plan was not intended to stand alone--it would prove unsuccessful if allowed to do so. Installation of these barriers would be preceded by an intensified conventional interdiction campaign throughout South Vietnam, Laos, and particularly NVN. The enemy logistics and personnel system would have to be interdicted to the maximum extent possible, long before they encountered the barriers. The latter would be just one more impediment to the enemy movement, and would in no way lessen the requirement to interdict the enemy as far up into his own territory as possible. 48/

The barrier plan was based on certain major assumptions. These were: 49/

> 1. The RLG and GVN would agree to the barrier and increased interdiction concepts, insofar as their own territorial boundaries were concerned;

2. Recognizing a relocation-of-population requirement, the GVN would expedite actions for acquisition of real estate;

3. Certain essential research and development items would be developed, tested, manufactured, shipped, and stockpiled in South Vietnam, as soon as practicable;

4. Enlarged existing programmed MACV requirements called for additional equipment, materiel, and shipping arrangements; and

5. Combat, combat support, and combat service support forces would be added to programmed MACV requirements, with minimum essential combat and combat support forces being obtained from its resources. These forces would secure the initial area of operations, including LOC cantonments, ports, and construction sites during the preparatory phases.

According to ACS, J-3, MACV, Maj. Gen. John C. F. Tillson, III, if these assumptions were invalid, then successful implementation of the plan in the time-frame involved was questionable. Aware that MACV advocated adoption of a realistic approach to the barrier development--based on avoidance of an inflexible time schedule--General Tillson stated that the Commander should be permitted to establish the pace of development based on his continuing assessment of the overall situation and availability of resources. 50/

Under the barrier plan, 7AF would be tasked to conduct an intensified aerial interdiction program in Laos. This included the selective use of aerial-delivered, area-denial weapons, and sensors, as they became available. In addition, 7AF was to be prepared to conduct tactical air operations, and aerial and ground reconnaissance.

A strong point/early warning barrier system would be installed in South Vietnam during May-November 1967. It would be continuous in the eastern 30 kilometers, extending from the South China Sea, and would be located as close as possible to the southern border of the DMZ. Strong points, mobile striking forces, and supporting fire elements would be located behind the continuous barrier. A series of strong points and defile barriers would be located in strategic areas in the western mountainous area, extending from the early warning barrier to Laos. 51/

To complement existing interdiction operations, a selective use of air-delivered, area-denial munitions, and sensors would be made in Laos. It would commence as soon as munitions, sensors, and delivery systems were available--no later than April 1968. This action would not be treated in isolation of the total war effort; it would complement the strong point/ early warning barrier system.

Under the barrier plan, infiltration routes would be interdicted by air and ground-delivered mines and detection devices. The interdiction routes would be covered by airstrikes, Nike Hercules surface-to-surface missiles (if available), and artillery within range. Lucrative targets would be selected, based on intelligence, and maximum power would be applied. This would include B-52 strikes, ground exploitation teams, and tactical air-delivered conventional munitions. 52/

Four distinct phases were envisioned for this plan with Phase I accomplished from November 1966 through 30 April 1967. During this phase, the Air Force would carry out increased reconnaissance and intelligence activities to identify infiltration routes. In addition, the Air Force would carry out increased air interdiction sorties in accordance with over-all priorities. Phase II, 1 May through 30 July 1967, would see a continuation of air interdiction. The Phase III period, 1 August through 31 October 1967, would initiate the westward movement. Air interdiction would be continued, and special munitions and sensors would be used as they became available. The sustained phase (Phase IV) would start on 1 November 1967, with no specific ending date. During this phase, extensive use of air-delivered munitions and sensors would be made in Laos. 53/

Although lying across routes frequented by the majority of infiltrating enemy personnel, it was concluded that the proposed air-delivered barrier system would probably hamper but not significantly reduce nor block their penetration. It would significantly reduce enemy truck movement, however, into the Laotian Panhandle, and would probably force the enemy to increase his resupply by sea, through Cambodia, and by inland waterways. 54/

Area-Denial Weapons

On 21 January 1966, COMUSMACV informed higher commands that area and route denial weapons were among the most critical operational problems in the SEA theater. He recommended: (1) a concept for employment of such weapons as Gravel, Dragon Tooth, and Trip Wire mines; and (2) periodic reseeding to maintain maximum effectiveness of denial and disruption to enemy operations and logistics.

To be used most advantageously, these weapons should be disseminated along likely infiltration routes into the RVN and along withdrawal routes from there. Area dissemination was also needed in the Viet Cong/PAVN base area, and in assembly areas of South Vietnam. It might also be possible to include establishment of a narrow barrier of denied territory just within South Vietnam, under the area-denial weapons expansion program. This would cover major segments of the DMZ, the Laos-RVN border, and the Cambodia-RVN border south to the area in Tay Ninh Province, where density of population made further use undesirable. Further assessment of the logistics and operational effort required to seed and maintain the barrier was needed before use of area-denial weapons could be expanded to this degree. 55/

To meet these specifications, COMUSMACV gave the following desired weapons: they must be effective against people, animals, and trucks, and be suitable for dissemination by aircraft over extended areas. These dispensers had to be compatible with UH, B-52, tactical fighters, B-57, and A-1 aircraft, and should have a self-destruction capability with a variable of from seven to 30 days. For interim weapons, a self-neutralization capability would be acceptable in place of the self-destruction capability. It would be desirable to have an antidisturbance capability at the earliest practicable date. The capability to penetrate the jungle canopy was also needed to permit full tactical employment in SEA. 56/ COMUSMACV provided these comments and recommendations on specific area-denial weapons: 57/

Gravel (XM-22E1)

This weapon had excessive self-sterilization time. Also,

it lacked the antidisturbance feature and this would permit extensive relocation by the enemy. For these reasons COMUSMACV did not want XM-22E1.

Gravel (XM-27)

This weapon lacked the antidisturbance feature and also the self-sterilization time was very short. Both these factors made it useful only as an interim capability, pending the availability of a more effective weapon. COMUSMACV recommended that this weapon be deployed to South Vietnam as early as possible.

Dragon Tooth

This weapon also was found acceptable only as an interim measure for the same reasons as Gravel types. COMUSMACV desired the early deployment of Dragon Tooth to use in conjunction with Gravel XM-27.

Trip Wire Mines

COMUSMACV wanted emphasis and priority on the development and production of this weapon, since it was believed to have the most effective potential. He wanted its development and production to include the capability of jungle canopy penetration and the self-destruction capability variable to be improved from seven to 30 days. The limited life-version was wanted as soon as it was available and the improved version was to follow as soon as possible.

COMUSMACV considered selected portions of four primary infiltration routes and five war zones/Viet Cong base areas (which were approximately 25 by 50 miles in area) as possible initial locations of employment for these mines. Considerations for use of the Trip Wire Mine were as follows: [58/]

> "The war zones/Viet Cong base areas would be seeded around their peripheries (150 miles) with a 3,800-foot wide strip of Trip Wire Mine. It would take five B-52s with loads totaling 272,000 mines to do the job. Approximately 329,000 mines would be required per area per month. The interior of each area would receive

> random seeding of strips 3,800 feet wide, which would vary in length and density."

Primary Infiltration Routes

It was envisioned that each of the four primary infiltration routes would be seeded in strips that averaged 3,000 feet long and 300 feet wide. Equal amounts of Dragon Tooth and Gravel would be utilized--approximately 11,520 mines were estimated to be required on a daily basis for each route. COMUSMACV wanted tactical fighters and the B-52 and B-57 aircraft to deliver the initial Trip Wire, Gravel, and Dragon Tooth weapons, with subsequent expansion including the UH and A-1 aircraft.

In June, CINCPAC authorized employment of ADLMs in SEA, and also established requirements for data collection and reporting procedures. In July, however, CINCPAC suspended employment of these weapons, pending a revaluation of safety hazards. The employment of the ADLM weapons system in SEA had aroused concern over its vulnerability to small arms fire, the lack of an emergency "drop safe" feature, and the questionable sterilization aspects of the mines. The suspension was subsequently canceled, and employment of ADLMs was authorized if certain restraints were observed and employment was initially conservative. [59]

The use of ADLMs was viewed as being more flexible and wider than the point interdiction technique, since it was not nearly as dependent on suitability of terrain as a choke point, and could capitalize on the element of surprise. Furthermore, with the exception of buried mines, it was an area-denial weapon. Plans for employment of ADLMs called for as varied and unique an approach as possible, to catch the enemy by surprise and complicate his task of devising countermeasures.

Various delivery patterns and mixes of mines were to be used, and random but highly selective areas would be mined, using variable seeding schedules to prevent development of a predictable pattern. In some instances, ADLMs would be seeded around and on interdiction points to discourage road repair or bypassing. They would also be used independently along segments of roads to damage, impede, and harass enemy traffic, and cause exploitable blockups of vehicles. Except for air-delivered anti-vehicle mines, which could cause interdiction and destruction of passing vehicles, the use of ADLMs was considered basically a harassment technique, although they could also cause some damage and casualties. 60/

Dispensing of ADLMs in Laos and SVN might have sensitive political implications, which could restrict the use of these munitions in some areas. Approval and coordination with the appropriate government would be required for mining operations. The research and development of desired features in ADLMs and sensor equipment might also be limiting factors. As of late November, the munitions and equipment did not possess the capabilities incorporated in previous planning. It had been based on items considered within the present state of the art; however, additional development and certification had to be accomplished prior to implementation of the plan. 61/
Specific limiting factors were as follows:

- The F-4 aircraft had not been certified to carry some of the munitions planned for utilization.

- Lack of a self-destruction feature on ADLMs might at some later date hinder friendly force entry into the mined area.

- Current Gravel, Dragon Tooth, and WAAPM dispensing systems were designed for low-altitude delivery. This dictated that mining operations be conducted under VFR conditions.

- Defoliation operations might be limited by weather, since they had to be conducted at low-altitude and were thus limited by minimum ceilings and visibilities.

- Traffic sensors currently suitable for planned operations were not airdroppable. The requirement for ground emplacement of these sensors would limit coverage and detection capability.

- The lack of an antitamper feature on traffic sensors might allow the enemy to "spoof" the detection system by repositioning.

COMUSMACV reported that the following percentage of munitions were used in-country in October: CBU-24 - 10 percent; Gravel (30-day life) - 10 percent; Button bomblets - 100 percent; Dragon Tooth (life of 1 - 3 days) - 100 percent. COMUSMACV stated that he preferred Dragon Tooth over Gravel for airdelivered barrier operations for several reasons. Handling and dispensing were simplified, it had increased power, and a thorough sterilization feature. The problem was nonattainability of the necessary 30 - 60-day life for Dragon Tooth. COMUSMACV felt that this might necessitate a larger quantity use of Gravel, at least until the long-life Dragon Tooth requirements could be met. 62/

The Aerial Delivered Land Mine System (ADLMS) was initiated on 26 December. The dispensing aircraft were followed by two UH-1Bs to provide suppressive fire and one UH-1D was on station as a recovery ship. The target area was under 48-hour surveillance by an O-1 aircraft. The mines were placed on the exit from a Vietnamese town to assist in sealing and subsequent searching of the village. Five of the eight sorties incurred malfunctions of the dispensing system and one sortie aborted due to this cause. 63/

Herbicide Operations

The effectiveness of herbicide operations had been proved by 1966, and the program was significantly expanded. Crop destruction operations had started in 1962, as part of the effort to weaken the Viet Cong by denying them certain sources of food supply. Defoliation operations began on an experimental basis in 1961, and were carried out in Viet Cong havens and along friendly lines of communications, bases, and installations. 64/

The defoliation program, Operation RANCH HAND, was extended in December 1965, in an effort to improve surveillance of the Ho Chi Minh Trail network, which covered an area of approximately 5,600 square miles of dense foliage. The 7AF was tasked with the entire program of target selection, development, reconnaissance, and operations.

Two C-123 aircraft and crews were deployed to Da Nang Air Base to begin the program. Each C-123B configured for defoliation usage was capable of laying a swath 14 kilometers in length and 80 meters in width. These dimensions produced a deposition rate of approximately three gallons of defoliant per acre of ground covered. 65/

Although the most effective time for application was during the growing season, this generally coincided with the wet season, which prevented maximum aircraft utilization. Under ideal climatic conditions, the first signs of kill could be seen after 24 - 48 hours. After six weeks, the sprayed area would appear barren and the vertical visibility would have improved 40 - 70 percent. The chemical did not poison the soil, and as a result regrowth could occur in the form of new grass and scrub after a period of four to six months. [66/]

Pink Rose

In September 1965, CINCPAC recommended to the JCS that an immediate requirement be established to develop a capability to destroy by fire large areas of forest and jungle growth in SEA. The request was approved and a test operation was conducted at Chu Pong Mountain near Pleiku. Burning of the area was accomplished on 11 March 1966, by B-52 strikes (Hot Tip I and II). The area selected had previously been defoliated, and incendiaries were dropped to ignite the area to be burned. Although the operation produced less than optimum results, the decision was made to conduct a full-scale controlled testing program in 1967, under the code name Pink Rose. The three targets selected for the test lay within War Zones "C" and "D". [67/]

During the period August - December 1966, selected areas were to be defoliated twice by C-123 aircraft, using orange or white herbicide dispensed from standard dispensers. Selected areas were to be resprayed, using blue desiccant approximately ten days before ignition. The selected areas would then be bombed by B-52 aircraft using M-35 Incendiary Cluster Bombs. The ensuing forest fire was expected to consume the dried vegetation and denude the target sufficiently to deny its use as a safe haven. The first target was ignited on 19 January 1967 with qualified success. The target area was accurately saturated by the ignition munitions, but did not produce the "fire storm" desired due to weather conditions. 68/

In October 1966, COMUSMACV requested permission to defoliate the northern sector of the DMZ and adjacent infiltration routes in NVN. The JCS forwarded the recommendation to the SECDEF on 10 November, but permission to defoliate the northern part of the DMZ was withheld pending results in the southern DMZ. MACV was tasked with conducting the qualitative assessment of the southern DMZ defoliation operation. 69/

There was some concern that the defoliation program in the southern portion of the DMZ might inadvertently result in spraying north of the provisional military demarcation line. The Secretary of State felt, however, that positive control of defoliation operations, and skillful handling of the public relations aspects of the program would keep any unfavorable reactions within manageable limits. 70/

The crop destruction and defoliation programs were controversial from their inception and subject to frequent evaluations. A study prepared by the MACV Combined Intelligence Center in July 1966, concluded that "at the present time, the advantages to the Allied forces from both programs significantly outweighed the disadvantages. Moreover, this favorable balance should support a considerable acceleration of the programs." 71/

The study further concluded that while limited scale crop destruction had not significantly affected overall VC food supplies, it had "caused logistical difficulties, diversions of manpower, some deterioration of morale, and at least temporary food shortages in the target areas...." It pointed out that the impact of the operations in target areas probably had adversely affected the goal of gaining popular support for the GVN but in nontarget areas, no significant impact had been apparent. 72/

Defoliation operations had been generally effective in increasing security of friendly installations and the lines of communication, and in causing limited disruption of the Viet Cong movement. Resentment toward the U.S. and GVN, caused by the unintentional destruction of civilian crops, was a serious problem, especially since many of the affected persons did not live under VC control. Conclusions of the study, however, showed that advantages of the program outweighed the disadvantages. 73/

The expanded herbicide program resulted in a shortage of herbicide and aircraft during the latter part of the year. In December, COMUSMACV requested CINCPAC's assistance in obtaining revised herbicide requirements. The original requirement of 5.62 million gallons for Fiscal Year (FY) 1967, was revised upward to 6.44 million. The FY 1968 requirements of 8.44 million gallons were increased to 11.9 million gallons, and aircraft requirements were increased from 18 to 24. COMUSMACV pointed out that curtailment of the current program to the level dictated by the shortages would cause an unacceptable impact upon military operations. 74/

To maintain the highly effective herbicide program at the required operational level, COMUSMACV recommended that DOD consider all sources of herbicide to obtain the needed quantities. He suggested that consideration be given to plant expansion, diversion from commercial markets, and offshore procurement. He also recommended that DOD research available vegetation and grass control products that might be substituted for orange or white agents for ground spray operations. 75/

Project Popeye

A Weather Modification program for selected areas of Laos, subsequently known as Project Popeye, was proposed by JCS on 10 August. COMUSMACV and CINCPAC concurred in the proposal and recommended that it be carried out in selected TIGER HOUND areas. JCS granted approval on 1 September and the execute order was issued on 17 September. 76/

JCS approved the project to extend the rainy season by cloud seeding in Laos, as a means of denying the enemy vehicular LOCs. According to intelligence sources, there was a significant movement of enemy supplies and personnel through the Se Kong watershed and the peripheral mountainous areas. Vehicular traffic was a frequently used method of transportation, but it was considerably hampered by poor road conditions caused by inclement weather. It was hoped that the cloud seeding project would cause further deterioration of the infiltration route. 77/

The prime objective of Project Popeye was to tailor the cloud seeding techniques developed by the Naval Ordnance Test Station, China Lake, California, to the unique meteorological, terrain, and operational conditions that existed in the particular area, and then conduct an operational evaluation of the concept. It was estimated that the initial portion, Phase IA, would take ten days, consisting of preliminary reconnaissance flights over operational areas, and some trial cloud seedings conducted for training and proof testing of operations techniques and aircraft. Phase 1B would last approximately 35 days and would consist of 50 case samples of randomly selected but controlled cloud seeding operations. 78/

Phase IB of Project Popeye commenced on 29 September and ended on 28 October. A 56-case sample was evaluated and more than 85 percent reacted in accordance with the project theory. There was also evidence of broader applications of weather modification such as cloud rain-out over the ocean to reduce precipitation of friendly forces, cloud dissipation by overseeding to improve visibility of friendly forces, and other applications based on tactical operations. In view of the success of Project Popeye, COMUSMACV recommended immediate full-scale implementation of the Popeye technique, to include these broader aspects. 79/

Based on experience gained during the test, 7AF wrote a Popeye plan for utilizing the technique as an adjunct to the weapons systems presently employed in the theater. The operations plan, based on Air Force control and execution of the entire operation, was approved by COMUSMACV and by JCS, who forwarded it to higher authority on 5 December, with approval to implement the project expected shortly. 80/

CLOSE AIR SUPPORT AND DIRECT AIR SUPPORT

Introduction

> "Vietnam has certainly demonstrated that tactical air is no longer relegated to a support function alone but is a capability in itself. While it has operated in extremely close support of and in close cooperation with the Army in destroying the enemy, it has also proven to be a force to be applied in itself against the opposition. Tactical air power will not win a war of the nature of that in Vietnam by itself, but it is clearly a vital element in the application of military forces...." 81/

During 1966, the Air Force provided significant close support to ground operations in the form of heavy strikes against enemy facilities and infiltration routes, extensive reconnaissance missions, and psychological warfare missions. The majority of ground operations being supported by close air support during 1966, were carried out to destroy enemy supply bases, reassembly, rehabilitation, and training areas, and to reduce effectiveness of command and control centers, as well as enemy operations.

Air operations penetrated areas which had long been under Viet Cong domination, and did much toward helping friendly forces in securing base areas. In 1966, the increase in air operations in South Vietnam prevented the enemy from fighting at the time and place of his choice; it succeeded in keeping him off-balance. The duration of these operations was also much longer--some continuing more than a month--as compared to a few days for an average operation in 1965. 82/

Since the U.S. goals were to help destroy enemy forces and wrest control from the communists, objectives for in-country use of airpower in 1966, emphasized assisting in expansion of cleared and secured areas in the RVN. These objectives had been divided into two catagories: (1) those of overall-area concern; and (2) those of individual Corps-area concern. Basically, the military objective of primary concern was to use airpower in helping provide sufficient security for expansion of GVN control and development in the heavily populated areas along the I and II Corps coastal plain, the Saigon area, and selected portions of the Mekong Delta.

To accomplish these goals, air sorties were required to help open and secure certain main roads, railroads, and waterways. Air resources also helped the Corps to defend outlying governmental centers, which were significant from a political or population viewpoint. Another mission of air was to help destroy or neutralize enemy forces in these areas. [83]

Support of the in-country effort remained the high priority task in the conduct of air operations in SEA during 1966. Airpower was highly effective throughout RVN in support of major ground actions and numerous small operations. During the year, 7AF units supported 81 major U.S. ground actions--14 in I Corps, 20 in II Corps and 47 in III Corps. [84]

Close air support in South Vietnam (with the exception of the Marine effort), was coordinated and controlled through the Tactical Air Control Center at Tan Son Nhut. This was a joint USAF/VNAF agency subordinate to the Joint Operations Center (JOC), but responsible to 7AF and VNAF Headquarters. There were five DASCs subordinate to this organization, enabling

FAC FLIES daily patrol
Figure 9

the TACC to operate on the principle of centralized direction and limited decentralized execution.[85/]

In RVN operations, all targets were approved by the province chief or through higher authority. Strikes would not be executed if identification of friendly forces was in doubt. Control by an air liaison officer (ALO), forward air controller (FAC), or MSQ-77 or ground control radars (TPQ-10) was required, with the exception that FACs were always required for strikes on villages. The presence of temples, pagodas, shrines, or other places of worship would negate approval of B-52 strikes. Immediate requests for airstrikes against targets, other than close support of ARVN/FW forces under direct attack and engaged in specified operations, would not be honored if the possibility of friendly casualties existed. Strikes not associated with a specified military operation required positive identification and RVN military/political authorities approval.[86/]

An analysis of close and direct air support utilized with ground troops during a three-month period (mid-March through mid-June) showed that 15 percent of the 985 operations conducted received air support. Thirty-two percent of the 366 operations that had enemy contact received air support. Search-and-destroy type operations represented more than 80 percent of all operations and 91 percent of those received air support.[87/]

Major Ground Operations

The following examples illustrate how airpower was used in some of the major ground operations during 1966:

Operation MASHER/WHITE WING

Operation MASHER/WHITE WING covered the 1st Air Cavalry participation in a joint US/ARVN/ROK operation, which was the largest to take place up to that time (February 1966). It was conducted along the coastal area in the vicinity of Bong Son, from 24 January to 6 March. The air support furnished was extensive and, in many instances, provided the necessary margin for overcoming enemy resistance. More than 1,100 Air Force, Navy, Marine, and VNAF strike sorties were flown, with nearly 2,000 tons of ordnance expended. In addition, night illumination was provided by USAF C-123s (Smokey Bear) and C-47 flareships, with fire support from Dragon AC-47s. Airlift support by the USAF continued throughout the operation, and for the first time, C-130s were used for in-theater close logistic support. More than 1,000 tons of supplies and equipment were flown into Bong Son by C-123s and C-130s. Ground forces support material was also airlifted to other points, where it could be transshipped by ground lines of communication to the area of operation. [88]

A Shau Special Forces Camp

The A Shau Special Forces Camp, located near the Laotian border in I Corps, came under a heavy Viet Cong/PAVN assault at 0200 hours on 9 March 1966. Due to adverse weather conditions, only 29 sorties could be flown in support of A Shau during the daylight hours (17 by USAF, 10 by USMC, and 2 by VNAF). Poor weather also prevented airstrikes during the night. On 10 March, 210 sorties were flown.

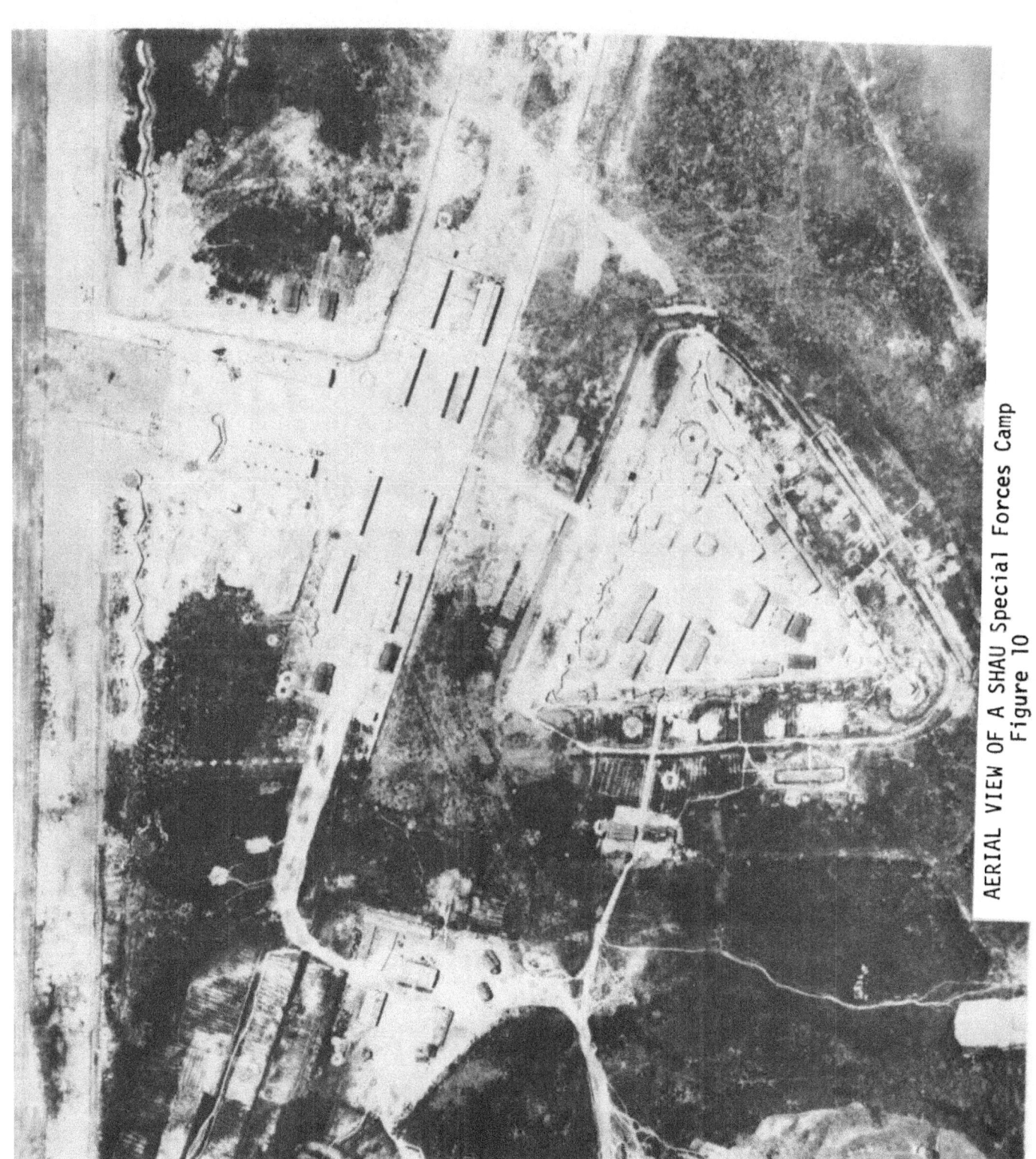

AERIAL VIEW OF A SHAU Special Forces Camp
Figure 10

Weather conditions impeded effectiveness of these strikes and forced aircraft to low altitudes where their vulnerability was increased. Despite desperate efforts of the defenders to hold A Shau, it was decided the situation was hopeless. Withdrawal from the camp became necessary, and on the evening of 10 March, U.S. Marine helicopters evacuated 69 wounded personnel.

U.S. Special Forces personnel suffered 100 percent casualties--5 killed and 12 wounded. In addition to ground casualties, there were three U.S. aircrew members killed and five reported missing. It was estimated that the Viet Cong lost about 300 to ground fire and an estimated 400 killed by airstrikes. The loss of A Shau was a substantial victory for the enemy, yet it was evident that without airpower there would have been no survivors. The fall of A Shau again demonstrated the need for a viable method of all-weather strike support. (See CHECO study, "Night Close Air Support in the RVN," 15 Mar 67.)

A B-52 raid was conducted at A Shau using CBU munitions on 19 March. Tactical airstrikes against enemy position at A Shau continued the next week, with aircraft strafing and bombing the enemy-held installations of this former Special Forces Camp. In a message to 7AF, the Commander, MACV, General William C. Westmoreland, said:[89]

> "...The air support provided by Marine and Air Force units at the recent battle of A Shau Special Forces Camp was equal to any in aviation history. The repeated heroic deeds of the transport, fighter and helicopter crews and forward air controllers, accomplished under extremely adverse conditions,

the utmost credit on the crews themselves and their respective services...."

Operation HAWTHORNE

Operation HAWTHORNE was conducted in Kontum Province during 2-21 June in a joint 101st Airborne Division/1st Air Cav Div/42d ARVN/CIDG effort. The initial objective of this operation was the relief of elements of the 42d ARVN Regiment at Toumorong, where intelligence indicated at least an enemy regiment. Before the operation ended, major contact was established with this Viet Cong regiment, and tactical air played a key role in handing the enemy a major defeat.

In Operation HAWTHORNE there were 250 immediate air sorties flown, compared to only 185 preplanned. This was a reversal of the usual pattern, and an indication of the flexibility of tactical air as organized in RVN, under the Tactical Air Control System. When major contact was made on 7 June 1966, airstrikes were being delivered in less than 30 minutes. The operation was supported by 445 tactical air sorties, which dropped 338.3 tons of ordnance, and 39 B-52 sorties, which dropped 702 tons of bombs. The B-52 strike made on 3 June 1966, came at a critical time and was credited with "crumbling" enemy resistance. In Operation HAWTHORNE, around-the-clock airstrikes also were conducted at night and in poor weather through the use of the Combat Skyspot radar bombing system. 90/

Operation EL PASO

Operation EL PASO was a major ground campaign conducted in the III

Corps Tactical Zone by the 1st Infantry Division, in conjunction with III Corps ARVN forces. There were five major engagements during the three-month campaign which began in May. All of them resulted in clear-cut victories for the friendly forces and in three of these, tactical airpower was the decisive factor. During the five major battles, the Air Force provided a total of 347 strike sorties, of which 225 were immediates. Strike and FAC aircraft were subjected to intense enemy ground fire but despite numerous hits, none were downed. The enemy suffered a confirmed loss of 779 KIA and a probable loss of more than 1,000 KIA. In commending the Air Force for their role during Operation EL PASO, Maj. Gen. William E. DePuy, the Commanding General, 1st Infantry Division, stated:

> "...Extremely close and accurate air support was accomplished under almost impossible weather conditions. The target area was obscured by a 200 to 400 foot ceiling. The FAC's talked the fighters through their deliveries and their support undoubtedly saved two infantry companies...."

General DePuy also made reference to this battle when he stated that there would be "occasions in the future in which we will wish to bring napalm and bombs in close to our own troops if in our opinion it will save lives in the long run." For this reason, he strongly requested that "no restrictions or inhibitions be permitted to interfere with the close air support of the 1st Infantry Division, and that no pressure be placed on air liaison officers nor forward air controllers...." 91/

Tactical air played many roles in the EL PASO operation. On more than one occasion, the 1st Infantry Division was entirely dependent upon air lines of communication during the operation. Tactical airlift provided over 1,650 C-130 sorties and 5,000 C-123 sorties, delivering over 30,700 troops and 19,500 tons of cargo. 92/

Operation ATTLEBORO

Operation ATTLEBORO, executed between 14 September and 26 November 1966, included in its area of operations, the northern three-quarters of Tay Ninh Province, the known location of the Central Office South Vietnam (COSVN), Headquarters of the National Front for the Liberation of South Vietnam (NFLSVN), and the main base of the Viet Cong 9th Division. From 1 to 25 November 1966, a total of 1,629 strike sorties, including 485 immediates, were flown; they expended 11,757.3 tons of ordnance. Tactical airlift also played an important role throughout the operation. C-123 Providers flew 2,712 sorties, while the C-130 Hercules contributed an additional 602 sorties. These aircraft transported 8,902 tons of cargo and 11,403 passengers, making a grand total of 10,270 tons of cargo and passengers airlifted between 18 October and 26 November. 93/

During the two and a half month period of Operation ATTLEBORO, 1,106 Viet Cong were confirmed killed in action by body-count. Hundreds of the enemy dead were estimated carried away from the battlefields, and additional hundreds may have been killed in the numerous B-52 strikes. In one case, 30 enemy dead were found in a trench—all without wounds—killed by bomb concussion. In another instance, a bomb made a direct hit on a battalion command post, cutting all communications and killing 13 enemy personnel.

The COSVN Headquarters was reportedly hit by B-52 strikes, and these strikes were credited with killing some cadre members and destroying tremendous quantities of documents, supplies, and equipment. Friendly losses were relatively low for an operation of this size, with 115 KIA and 494 WIA. [94]

Tactical airstrike results, including structures destroyed and damaged, increased during the first part of the year, then gradually decreased. This was not an indication of decreased effectiveness, but was caused by a decrease in the number of targets of that type available or struck, and also the inability to observe results in many instances. Cumulative results measured during the year showed that more than 100,000 structures and nearly 4,000 sampans were destroyed, and there were more than 2,800 secondary explosions recorded. During the year there were 71 strike aircraft lost due to combat in-country by USAF, USMC, USN, and VNAF. [95]

ARC LIGHT

The ARC LIGHT program played an increasingly important role in SEA air operations during 1966. Expansion of the Guam-based heavy bomber strike effort was reflected in an ever-increasing monthly sortie rate applied against a constantly growing geographical area. By the end of the year, B-52 strikes had been conducted in the DMZ, Laos, the Cambodian border area, and the North Vietnamese border areas, as well as in South Vietnam. The number of B-52s increased from 30 to 50, and during the year they flew 5,248 sorties, expending 100,074 tons of munitions. [96]

The primary purpose of the B-52 strike program was the destruction of command and control systems and personnel, supply facilities, base camps, training facilities, harassment of LOCs, and psychological effects. Targets were located in enemy-controlled areas, where friendly ground forces had been unable to operate frequently. No set targeting criteria could be used, since each target was subject to individual examination, nor were targets selected for ARC LIGHT strikes generally suitable for attacks by tactical forces. 97/

These procedures were employed for ARC LIGHT planning and operational control. The JCS allocated the number of monthly ARC LIGHT sorties, and CINCPAC had the responsibility of approving the strikes within the purview of his authority, while others were referred to JCS. (ARC LIGHT strikes in Laos required approval of JCS and CINCPAC, and these approvals were given only on concurrence of the American Ambassador in Vientiane.) The development and justification of each B-52 strike was the responsibility of COMUSMACV, who also obtained the necessary clearances from the host country. CINCSAC provided the force requirements to carry out ARC LIGHT strike missions. The responsibility of the Commander, 7AF, was essentially one of coordinating the in-country air activity around the ARC LIGHT strike. In addition, he would provide air defense and escort drops and follow-up reconnaissance, when they were required. The in-country TACC was responsible for coordinating and fragging the air activity affected by an ARC LIGHT mission in-country. When out-of-country resources were utilized (CAP/ESCORT for northern missions), the in-country TACC coordinated with the out-of-country TACC who did the actual fragging. 98/

All of these functions, reconnaissance, escort, follow-up strikes, etc., were inseparably related to the B-52 function. In the opinion of the Commander 7AF, B-52s were thus essentially an extension of current tactical operations and needed to be more precisely managed to minimize mutual interference, while getting the most security and effectiveness from the strike force. As Air Component Commander, the 7AF Commander was charged by COMUSMACV with responsibility for all USAF operations in the MACV area, but he did not participate in planning for B-52 operations before receiving notification of a decision to make the strike.

With the expansion of the ARC LIGHT program during 1966, wider participation by 7AF in B-52 operations appeared even more desirable. The 7AF Commander pointed out in a message to Headquarters USAF on 23 September, the B-52 operations had now expanded to such an extent that the original ARC LIGHT system was no longer applicable. He recommended that target selection by MACV be continued, but that 7AF exercise operational control of B-52 forces during the execution phase. This would also allow a smoother integration into daily air operations, and would provide better coordination in follow-up visual BDA and fighter strikes. The Director of the MACV Combat Operations Center, who was responsible for B-52 strikes, concurred that responsibility should be passed to the Air Force Component Commander. He was becoming concerned because of the magnitude of the program and MACV's ability to accommodate it without undue expansion of facilities and personnel. 99/

Headquarters USAF proposed, however, that the current SACLO at Tan Son Nhut be increased to a SAC ADVON. It was to be attached to the COMUSMACV Deputy for Air and would assume responsibility for operational planning. This would satisfy the requirement to streamline and improve the targeting, tasking, and approval and coordination procedures, as they pertained to B-52 operations. At the same time, this arrangement would provide better integration of ARC LIGHT into the overall SEA air operations, and insure that qualified personnel made the force allocation; i.e., the determination of whether strategic or tactical forces attacked a specified target. There were to be no changes in the present SAC command relationship in providing ARC LIGHT support. CINCSAC and COMUSMACV (with one minor exception) agreed with the USAF proposal for the ADVON, and it was to be implemented in 1967. 100/

Reaction Time

In anticipation of an enemy offensive during the southwest monsoon, COMUSMACV stated in May that it was essential that "we gear our reaction capability to offset this weather factor to the maximum extent." The 7AF had already increased appreciably its all-weather air support and bombing capabilities, with the deployment of the MSQ-77 radar units, operation of ground long-range weather detection radar, the B-66B Pathfinder Buddy Bombing System, the F-4C UHF/DF homing capability, and the X-band radar beacons. In addition, COMUSMACV believed that more B-52 spoiling raids should be employed on a timely basis. He wanted the reaction time between the detection of the threat and the time on target reduced to the minimum. One answer to the problem would be to have ARC LIGHT strikes conducted through use of the MSQ-77. By using this system, B-52 aircraft could be diverted in flight to targets developed by the latest intelligence. Another possible solution would be to stage B-52 aircraft at bases closer to RVN. 101/

As an interim solution, COMUSMACV recommended to CINCPAC that six Guam-based B-52 aircraft be placed on continuous alert, ready to react immediately with a minimum of briefing and target study requirements. This recommendation was implemented on 1 July 1966, when the 4133d Bomb Wing (SAC) at Andersen AFB, Guam, was ordered to place six B-52 aircraft on continuous alert. At the same time, six KC-135s were placed on standby alert at Kadena AB, Okinawa. The first Quick Reaction Strike in RVN utilized the MSQ-77 Combat Skyspot bombing system; it was successfully carried out on 6 July in support of the 1st Brigade of the 1st Air Cavalry Division operations in Phu Yen Province. 102/

The question of forward-basing B-52s to cut reaction time from Guam was also discussed in-depth during the year. It was estimated that through forward-basing of these aircraft, the 800 sorties per month scheduled for 1967, could be carried out by 50 B-52s, as compared to 70 B-52s required if operations were to be conducted from Guam. CINCPAC listed U-Tapao, Thailand; Kadena, Okinawa; Mac Tan; Clark; and Ching Chuan Kang in Taiwan, as possible bases for the ARC LIGHT forces. CINCPAC felt that the U-Tapao location had many advantages. It was not only near to the target area, but a nearby contractor capability could carry out rapid construction on support requirements. All of these locations presented certain political problems, but none of them appeared insurmountable. No final determination on a forward site had been made at the end of the year. 103/

Information Leaks

There was considerable concern at all echelons regarding the possibility of information leaks to the enemy on planned ARC LIGHT strikes. Reports received from defectors, ralliers, and prisoners indicated the receipt of advance warning of pending B-52 strikes against their units. Radio transmission was one of the likely sources of information compromise; therefore, to avoid future jeopardization, increased communications security including encrypting and encoding, was one of the solutions effected. 104/

Tiny Tim

Another problem was encountered when the ARC LIGHT program expanded northward into the DMZ, and the B-52s entered areas of possible SAM emplacements. Toward the end of the year, it became necessary to provide support for ARC LIGHT forces to enable them to operate within these areas. The Timy Tim support plan incorporated a combined ELINT search using fighter support aircraft to uncover definite SAM threat signals or observation of a SAM launch. 105/

ARC LIGHT Assessment

The problem of evaluating qualitative and quantitative effects of the ARC LIGHT program persisted throughout 1966, due to the nature of the targets struck, the terrain and foliage restrictions, and the recognized VC policy of keeping results of strikes hidden.

While the most reliable means for evaluating effectiveness of each B-52 strike was by ground follow-up, the nonavailability of ground forces, or inaccessability of the target made this method impractical in most instances. Photo interpretation reports aided by providing a simple count of a certain number of craters being "in" and "out." Exposure of tunnels and dugouts in facilities identifiable from larger scale photography usually confirmed validity of these targets and evidence of exploded ordnance in the vicinity. [106/]

The B-52 operations had the unqualified support of COMUSMACV, who considered them productive in contributing to the defeat of the VC. In analyzing the effectiveness of the ARC LIGHT program, COMUSMACV stated in April that it had: (1) hindered initiation of the third phase of insurgency warfare; (2) precluded large scale troop concentrations; (3) disrupted the logistical support organizations; (4) affected the VC economic support base; and (5) alienated noncombatants from the VC. [107/]

Ground commanders were also generally unanimous in their praise of the B-52s. Maj. Gen. Fred C. Weyand, Commanding General, II FFV, typified this feeling when he stated: [108/]

> "...We had wonderful luck with the B-52 strikes. We got 18 strikes and the 25th and 1st Division used them like close air support or long range artillery. A B-52 strike severely damaged COSVN headquarters and another landed directly on the 9th Division headquarters. These strikes severely disrupted the enemy's command chain...."

The 7AF Commander observed that when heavy bombers had been used for close support in the past, there had always been large logistical concentrations or multidivision attacks, however, these factors did not prevail in the SEA theater of operations. He, therefore, pointed out:[109/]

> "...we have to be careful about over-stating the case for B-52's in this environment. I do not believe we should look at B-52's like fighter forces for quick reaction. The problem of loading, briefing, navigation, terrain unfamiliarity, coordination with other air and ground operations all tend to stylize bomber operations to a degree...."

In further elaboration of this theme, the 7AF Directorate of Intelligence stated in June:[110/]

> "...In summary, evaluation of the effectiveness of B-52 strikes remains an unknown quantity. The merits of employing such a strategic weapons system against the types of targets that have been selected are still debatable. The expenditure of ordnance by B-52's does not appear to be justified either on the basis of target selection or on the basis of BDA which presumably should provide justification for subsequent B-52 strikes. Thus, several hundred tons of bombs are dropped into a small area, and are perhaps wasted, whereas the same tonnage could be parcelled out among a greater number of fighter bomber sorties tailored and directed against a wider spectrum of targets. Furthermore, in the latter instance there is a much better probability of acquiring meaningful BDA, and thus rendering a more substantive evaluation of effectiveness of Tactical Air Forces in this theater. There are proper targets for B-52 mass saturation attacks; but these no longer exist in-country. Whereas once such targets as base camps were considered suitable B-52 targets, they have now become so small as to warrant only tactical air strikes...."

RECONNAISSANCE

Interdiction and close air support were only two of the varied roles played by the Air Force. In the SEA theater, the Air Force's traditional reconnaissance mission acquired new dimensions. Reconnaissance included not only visual means, but also photographic, infrared, electronics, and communications intelligence. Since the majority of all reconnaissance in SEA was conducted by air, the term "recce" became identified as aerial reconnaissance. Airstrikes were developed mainly from the intelligence collected by Air Force means, and considerable imagination was displayed in evolving new ways to gain it. Some of these methods involved new equipment, but most were an adaptation of existing equipment to new environments. The overall requirements for reconnaissance in the SEA theater exceeded the historic ratio of recce workload to air-ground operations for all previous conflicts in which the U.S. had been involved. 111/

As of December 1965, the reconnaissance units in SEA had been divided three ways: geographically, for command control, and support. To provide the cohesive organization required for an expanding recce program, 7AF requested the formation of a tactical reconnaissance wing in SEA. PACAF approved the proposed organization and the 460th Tactical Reconnaissance Wing (TRW), Headquarters, Tan Son Nhut, was activated on 18 February 1966.

The wing was charged with responsibility for all SEA tactical and technical reconnaissance functions. Beginning with four squadrons, three photo interpretation cells and three detachments, the recce effort increased to two wings, two recce tech squadrons, eight reconnaissance squadrons, and three detachments. The aircraft inventory increased from 67 to 143 aircraft. As the buildup continued, the 460th TRW, composed of nine tactical flying squadrons, became the largest wing in Air Force history. The 7AF supported units located in RVN and the 13AF, with some 5AF assistance, supported the units located in Thailand.

Although all units were under operational control of 7AF, the logistical support presented cumbersome and difficult problems. Many of these problems were resolved by activation of the 432d TRW, Headquarters Udorn, on 18 September 1966, which was assigned to 13AF, with operational control exercised by 7AF. The Thailand squadrons of the 460th TRW were concurrently reassigned to the 432d TRW. 112/

Out-of-Country Recce

Blue Tree and Yankee Team were two major out-of-country recce operations which continued during 1966. With initiation of ROLLING THUNDER, the JCS granted CINCPAC authority to conduct Blue Tree, a reconnaissance program over North Vietnam, south of the 21st parallel and outside a 40-mile radius of Hanoi and Haiphong. Its purpose was to provide photo coverage to update target folders and develop future targets. The first Blue Tree mission was flown on 27 March 1965. Yankee Team, initially authorized by the JCS in May 1964, provided medium and low-level reconnaissance over Laos. 113/

CINCPACAF informed CINCPAC in August 1966, that an urgent requirement existed to revise current procedures governing conduct of out-of-country tactical reconnaissance to permit greater operational flexibility and increase sortie effectiveness. Blue Tree and Yankee Team recce requirements were managed by two distinct and separate recce programs. Accordingly, reconnaissance forces operating from Udorn, overflew Laos to and from higher priority areas of North Vietnam.

In many cases because of weather and/or tactical considerations, it would have been possible to reconnoiter Laos (Yankee Team) requirements en route from NVN, but under existing restrictions this potential could not be exploited. Consolidation of recce coverage of both areas would necessitate some changes in reporting procedures, but would result in increased sortie effectiveness. Dual fragging of Blue Tree missions into NVN and Laos began in October 1966. It provided better utilization of aircraft and crews, and in addition improved overall effectiveness of the recce effort. Primary targets remained in the Blue Tree area, while those in Laos were assigned as alternates. In December, out of 1,776 sorties attempted in North Vietnam, weather forced 159 to be diverted to the Yankee Team area. Under former restrictions, these 159 sorties would have been lost. 114/

Blue Springs

The 7AF also provided support for Blue Springs, which was a high altitude SAC photographic project, against northern North Vietnam and South China. In April, CINCPACFLT pointed out that the high loss of Blue Springs platforms meant a consequent loss of valuable coverage of those areas which were considered as high risk areas for Blue Tree photo reconnaissance. He noted that this adversely affected strike planning and strike execution.

For these reasons, CINCPACFLT felt that tactics and procedures should be developed which would enhance their survivability. He pointed out that the only one available.[120]

Organization

At the beginning of the year, the Commander, 7AF, had control of only a limited number of the airlift forces operating in his area of responsibility. The C-130 fleet and the aerial port units were assigned to units in other commands. On 3 May 1966, the Commander, 7AF, proposed that the in-country airlift structure be reorganized to include a troop carrier division assigned directly to 7AF. The air division would be composed of a wing of C-123s, a C-130 wing, a CV-2 wing, and an aerial port group. The proposal was accepted by CINCPAC, with the exception of the C-130 wing.[121]

The 834th Air Division and two of its units, the 483d Troop Carrier Wing (C-7A) and the 315th Air Commando Wing (C-123) were activated on 15 October 1966; the 2d Aerial Port Group was transferred from Japan to South Vietnam on 8 November 1966. The mission of the 834th Air Division was to provide sustained tactical airlift and maintenance of the air line of communication for all Free World Forces in SEA, by performing the following: air-land operations and resupply; airborne operations and resupply; and defoliation.[122]

Planning of the airlift operation and control of airlift resources was accomplished by the Airlift Control Center (ALCC) at Tan Son Nhut, and its 11 field extensions, the Airlift Control Elements. The Commander, 834th AD, stated that one of the most severe problems in command and control of the airlift fleet was the lack of adequate communications. The current

AIRLIFTING ARTILLERY to Field Forces
Figure 11

system did not provide sufficient information on aircraft movements, load status, airfield status, and all the data required to plan and execute the tactical airlift mission. Steps had been taken, however, to establish a SEAOR for a computerized command and control system built around a central computer located at the ALCC. [123/]

2d Aerial Port Group

The 2d Aerial Port Group, with a personnel strength of about 2,000, was responsible for providing terminal services support for all military airlift aircraft arriving and departing RVN. With headquarters at Tan Son Nhut, it had three aerial port squadrons located at major cargo generation points in RVN: the 8th Aerial Port Squadron at Tan Son Nhut, the 14th at Cam Ranh Bay, and the 15th at Da Nang. There were 39 detachments and operating locations assigned from these squadrons throughout Vietnam.

The aerial ports provided terminal services support, including loading and offloading of cargo and the processing of passengers. The three combat control teams in Vietnam provided air traffic control facilities and operations at remotely located austere airfields. The 2d Aerial Port Group also deployed mobility teams to assist with large unit moves. About 480,000 passengers each month or some 5 million passengers per year were handled through these terminals, which also accommodated nearly 1,300,000 tons of cargo yearly. Tan Son Nhut had handled more than 3,800 passengers in one day. In the 12 months ending 30 June 1966, Tan Son Nhut controlled twice the cargo handled by Chicago's O'Hare Airport - America's busiest air cargo airport. [124/]

The Commander, 834th AD, pointed out in January 1967, his awareness of a slight improvement in the material handling equipment maintenance area, but recognized that further improvement was necessary. He stated that an urgent need still existed for in-country or the peripheral base IRAN program for worn-out equipment; an AFLC maintenance team for on-the-spot repairs; and an improved spare support and component rebuild program. One of the primary factors contributing to the high out-of-commisssion rates on materials handling equipment was the inadequate aerial port facilities. Another factor detracting from aerial port capability was the congested ramp spaces. Airlift aircraft were sometimes forced to wait for a chance to park or even circle, while awaiting ramp space at some of the smaller strips. At other bases, cargo was processed in as many as three separate areas to accommodate all the port requirements. All of these factors contributed to excessive turnaround times. [125]

315th Air Commando Wing

The mission of the 315th Air Commando Wing was to operate and maintain the tactical and logistical airlift system within South Vietnam by performing the following: air-land resupply missions; airborne resupply missions; flare night illumination missions; and defoliation spray missions. The wing headquarters and two squadrons were located at Tan Son Nhut, with one squadron at Nha Trang, and another at Da Nang. The 18 U.E. defoliation Squadron, commonly known as "Ranch Hand," was stationed at Bien Hoa. The 315th Headquarters and one squadron were scheduled to move from Tan Son Nhut to Phan Rang in the near future. The C-123 limiting factor was insufficient aircrews, but crew manning was expected to improve slightly by early 1967.[126/]

C-130 Force

While in-country, the C-130 force came under operational control of the 834th AD, but overall command and supervision was exercised by Det 5 at Tan Son Nhut. The parent organization of Det 5 was the 315th Air Division, with headquarters at Tachikawa Air Base, Japan. The fleet consisted of 44 airplanes: 23 at Tan Son Nhut, 13 at Cam Ranh Bay and 8 at Nha Trang. The crews were provided on a rotation TDY basis for a period of 15 days.[127/]

Based on a review of the airlift system employed in Vietnam, COMUSMACV expressed his concern to CINCPAC in October, as to ability to support future planned tactical operations, while maintaining the required air line of communications. The concern was based on the CINCPAC forecast of total C-130 airlift shortages, the rapidly rising C-130 airlift requirement in Vietnam, and inadequacy of the present system to satisfy the current total intra-combat zone requirement. He stated that although the 315th AD provide 39 C-130s to meet July and August requirements of 38 aircraft, there was an average of 9.8 aircraft per day out of commission. He further stated that day-to-day operational rates varied from nearly 100 percent to a low of 50 percent. In reference to CINCPAC's opposition to basing C-130s in SVN, because of a lack of hard core maintenance, base overcrowding, and economic considerations, MACV said:

> "...These problems exist, however, the requirement also exists for a greater in-country maintenance capability to return non-productive C-130's to operational status in a minimum period. Non-flyable TDY aircraft still occupy ramp space but without the level of maintenance necessary for a quick turnaround. Overcrowding of other base facilities and economic inflationary pressures are problems that must be balanced against military necessity...."

He recommended, as a matter of urgency, that a C-130 wing be assigned to 7AF and based in Vietnam. Several advantages for basing a wing in Vietnam were cited: in-country maintenance capability; permanent aircrews oriented to SEA; establishment of a spare parts level based on SEA consumption rate; streamlined command channels and continuity of planning between users and operators.

The Chief, Western Transport Office, however, did not concur with COMUSMACV's proposal, on the basis that fragmentation of C-130 resources would hinder efficient management, and maximum utilization of available aircraft would not be achieved. CINCPACAF did not concur, also, because he considered the present C-130 route structure and in-country rotational concept, the best means of satisfying MACV/PACOM airlift requirements with present forces assigned.

Airlift deficits existed within the PACOM total requirements, but these deficits were absorbed in areas external to SEA, and the needs of the in-country war effort were being met. Existing deficits and requirements could be managed only if centralized control of the total C-130 assets were maintained. A withdrawal of four or six squadrons from the resources available to the total route structure would compound current deficits and would have a serious impact on the ability of the airlift system (PACAF and MAC) to support the overall PACOM war effort. Furthermore, the additional construction cost and piastre impact, associated with these deployments, would far outweigh any intangible aims which might be claimed for such basing. CINCPACAF, therefore, strongly recommended that the current airlift command/control arrangements be continued. [128]

A conference was convened at MACV on 10 November for the purpose of developing a position, based on the latest thinking of airlift personnel to counter the CINCPACAF/CINCPAC objections to in-country basing of C-130s. No decision was made at the meeting on whether to forward the points developed to CINCPAC, or await a more favorable time to reclama CINCPACAF's position. [129]

Project Red Leaf

On 6 April 1966, the Chiefs of Staff, U.S. Army and U.S. Air Force, concluded an agreement to transfer all CV-2 and C-7A assets and their control from the Army to the Air Force. The Joint Basic Plan, Project Red Leaf, required completion of actions to effect this agreement before the date of transfer on 1 January 1967. Accordingly, the 7AF Headquarters' planning provided the establishment of a troop carrier wing headquarters, six troop carrier squadrons, and appropriate maintenance and support units. The 6252d Operations Squadron (Red Leaf) was established as a holding unit of assignment for Air Force personnel, replacing Army personnel, pending the effective date of transfer. [130]

The major revision to the original 7AF plan was the relocation of squadrons from An Khe and Qui Nhon to Phu Cat. This was primarily due to the lack of facilities which would be available for Air Force use, although it was in accord with 7AF policy to position Air Force units on Air Force bases, whenever possible. When facilities could be made available to accommodate the two squadrons at Vung Tau, these likewise would be repositioned.

COMUSMACV's concurrence to the revised beddown proposal of 7AF was not received until 23 November 1966. The resulting short lead-time for required construction created a major problem area, which was further aggravated by unseasonably heavy rains, particularly in the Phu Cat area. The squadrons accomplished the moves on schedule, despite a shortage of facilities at Phu Cat and Cam Ranh Bay. All facilities programmed for the C-7A units were scheduled for completion on or before July 1967. 131/

Due to a shortage of pilots and equipment readiness, the C-7A squadrons did not attain a "C-1" rating on 1 January 1967. Of the 130 pilots required for a "fully combat-ready" rating, only 121 were on board as of that date. It was estimated, however, that a "C-1" rating could be attained by the spring of 1967. The shortage of aircraft (only 85 of the 96 authorized were assigned), and their poor condition, made it extremely difficult to meet the heavy flying schedule. This run-down condition appeared due to improper and inadequate maintenance, plus the lack of engine conditioning or corrosion control programs. 132/

Emergency Airlift Request Systems (EARS)

Prior to 1 November, normal procedures for the U.S. Army to request emergency and preplanned airlift were through each intermediate headquarters, beginning at battalion level to MACV Combat Operation Center. The requests were encoded and decoded at each level and, before forwarding them, they were evaluated as valid requirements. This system required as long as 12 hours for emergency requests and up to 72 hours for requests of priority one or lower. The ALCC did not receive any pre-alert as to pending emergency requests.[133/]

The programmed acquisition of the C-7A fleet by the Air Force on 1 January 1967 required 7AF to provide a means which would most satisfactorily meet the Field Commander's emergency battlefield airlift needs. It was thought that a communications net manned by qualified airlift personnel, at all levels of Army command down through the separate brigades, could best provide the desired response of emergency airlift. This would be accomplished in much the same manner as fighter support was currently provided through the Direct Air Support Net.[134/]

COMUSMACV withheld approval, until a test of the system was conducted in II and III Corps during 1 through 23 November 1966. The system received its most comprehensive test in III Corps during Operation ATTLEBORO. In this 26-day period, 126 emergency airlift requests were processed. The test was considered successful and with some modification, was approved by COMUSMACV.[135/]

The Commander, 7AF, stated in October that no major changes in the concept of operations of the C-7As were contemplated immediately after take-over. He believed it essential that a minimum of 30 days should elapse, before making any changes, so that USAF personnel could become thoroughly familiar with the complete CV-2 mission. After this period, changes could be accomplished gradually, which would provide more effective integration of the CV-2 fleet and yet insure the responsiveness required. 136/

The concept of operations advanced by the Commander, 7AF, for eventual employment of the CV-2 fleet, however, differed radically from the system used by the Army. If the 7AF plan were implemented, it had to function in a manner superior to the Army system. The U.S. Army field commanders were unanimously opposed to any changes and were suspicious and distrustful of the USAF system. While theoretically, the Air Force system was practical and effective, whether it would respond in actual execution remained to be tested or proved. Since the testing could not start until the Air Force took over control on 1 January 1967, 7AF planned to critically examine the system in great detail to identify flaws and correct deficiencies before the execution phase. 137/

PSYCHOLOGICAL WARFARE

The 5th Air Commando Squadron (ACS) effectively contributed to the intensified psychological warfare (psywar) effort during the year. Its mission was to provide in-country aerial support for psywar through loudspeaker broadcasts and leaflet dissemination. This squadron became fully operational on 15 December 1965, however, it had been activated on 8 August 1965, and was in place at Nha Trang by 8 November 1965, to provide USAF support in meeting increased psyops efforts.

The squadron received its first major assignment early in 1966, participating in Operation TET, the largest psychological warfare operation ever attempted in the Vietnam war. This was a nationwide, all-media campaign by U.S. and GVN agencies, to influence as many Viet Cong and their supporters as possible to rally to GVN control during 9-20 January, the New Year holiday season.

In this 12-day period, the 5th ACS flew 559 sorties in 1,347 hours of flying time, dropped more than 130 tons of leaflets, and broadcast more than 370 hours of taped messages. Nine aircraft were damaged by enemy ground fire and one man was wounded. All missions were flown as scheduled, however, and the campaign was an unqualified success. [138]

In addition to the normal day-in and day-out pacification mission, the 5th ACS also participated in all major tactical operations, such as NATHAN HALE, PAUL REVERE, VAN BUREN, JOHN PAUL JONES, HASTINGS, etc. In these operations, the aircraft were at the disposal of ground force commanders, and activities were coordinated with the controlling agency through continuous radio contact. This permitted them to broadcast messages to friendly or neutral villagers, or follow up on artillery strikes with surrender demands almost instantly. [139]

The effectiveness of 5th ACS operations was dramatically illustrated during Operation IRVING. A psyops aircraft flying north of Qui Nhon noted ground activity on a small island off the coast. They flew over the island and played a surrender tape. Approximately 30 minutes later several Viet Cong moved into the open with their hands raised. Army helicopters took them to a nearby camp with the psyops personnel following. They convinced the VC leader to make a tape and returned to the island to play the new tape until darkness. Sixty-six VC from that area returned to government control.140/

In addition to in-country psyops, the 5th Air Commando Squadron supported the program of leaflet drops over NVA infiltration routes. The program was designed to create anxiety among NVA infiltrators concerning their families in NVN, doubt of their own prospects for survival, and hopelessness of their mission during movement from NVN through Laos into SVN. In addition, 5th ACS aircraft were employed in the STEEL TIGER operational area of Laos, to conduct loudspeaker operations along the final stage of infiltration routes and in the RVN border areas.141/

During the initial months of operation, the 5th ACS developed tactics and coordinated procedures with the many agencies involved in psychological operations. At first, leaflet drops were made at 1,500 feet for coverage of large areas, and at 50 to 200 feet for smaller targets. Because of the intensity of small arms fire, the flights at low altitudes were abandoned in favor of fused bundles of leaflets. By dropping leaflet bundles fused to open at low altitude, it was possible to obtain the same accuracy with far less hazard from enemy ground fire. Also, leaflet chutes were designed and installed in the C-47s to improve coverage and reduce the work involved in mass leaflet drops.[142/]

The 5th ACS, with headquarters at Nha Trang, and operational detachments in each of the four CTZs, operated four C-47 and 17 U-10 aircraft fitted with loudspeaker systems having an effective audio range of 3,000 feet. By July, requirements forecasted for aerial psyops support were more than four times the original effort. As a result of increased support of combat operations, aircraft resources were being overextended, causing increased nonavailability due to excessive maintenance loads. Aircraft nonavailability resulted in losses of primary mission support to combat operations and impacted on the total psyops campaign, as well as on sector pacification efforts. Increasing demands to provide adequate support particularly affected the squadron's response capability to Quick Reaction strike requests normally generated at the engaged unit level.

Analysis by Headquarters, 7AF of 5th ACS operational data revealed 13,021 missions were requested during the period 9 May - 12 June 1966. Less than 100 of them could not be accomplished due to lack of aircraft. Of the more than 11,000 missions actually scheduled, only 142 were canceled due to maintenance problems, weather cancellations, and other reasons beyond squadron control.[143/]

In an effort to alleviate the problem of increased requirements from limited resources, the Commander, 7AF, proposed that the CTZ Propaganda Support Center (PSC) be more fully exploited through greater operational emphasis and expanded membership. CTZPSC members would include representatives not only from the Corps G-5 staff and psyops team, but from all ground forces, the local DASC, and 5th ACS Detachment. In this manner, the CTZPSC, meeting on a frequent and planned basis, could consolidate all targets and requirements, plan for the best utilization of available assets, and vastly increase utilization of the psyops force. 144/

Based on programmed increases in SVN psyops thru January 1967, the 7AF Commander determined that six additional C-47s, or equivalent cargo aircraft (CV-2s), would be required. A request to CINCPAC for additional aircraft was forwarded by him to JCS for approval within force requirements of FY 1966. In October, JCS directed the deployment of six C-47 aircraft to SVN. The C-47s were to undergo modification in CONUS, and were expected to be deployed not later than 15 January 1967. These six C-47s, combined with 20 O-2Bs, were to form a new air commando squadron, the 9th ACS, which was to be deployed to SVN by July 1967. As an interim measure, MACV directed that steps be taken to divert flying hours from other available USA/USAF/USMC/VNAF/ aircraft assets suitable for leaflet drop. 145/

The increased psyops effort, in which the 5th ACS played a notable role, was one of the many factors contributing to the success of the Chieu Hoi (open arms) program. A total of 20,242 persons rallied to the GVN during the year as compared to 11,124 in 1965. Throughout the year more than one and one-half billion leaflets were disseminated over SVN, 12,903 aerial psyop sorties were flown, and 7,537 hours of aerial loudspeaker time were used. 146/

The USAF also dropped 512,000,000 leaflets and large quantities of gifts over North Vietnam. The 7AF fragged 72 leaflet deliveries over North Vietnam, in addition to 61 deliveries accomplished by the wind-drift method. During the early part of the year, C-130s were fragged to fly directly over the southern portion of North Vietnam. The buildup of SAMS and antiaircraft weapons in this area caused a change in procedures. Aircraft began flying over Laos and coastal waters, depending on wind-drifts to distribute the leaflets over NVN.

Leaflet drops over the Red River Delta were accomplished by delivery aircraft flying in flights of four, with each carrying ten bombs whose individual capacity was 80,000 leaflets. These flights were supported by fighter aircraft. In order to avoid being hit in the highly defended Hanoi/Haiphong area, they employed a toss-bomb technique. The bomb canister utilized a timing device to release leaflets into the airstream at the optimum altitude. [147/]

An intelligence report on the effectiveness of the Fact Sheet leaflet campaign showed that Hanoi residents expected their city to be bombed, and anticipated that warnings would be provided by leaflets prior to such operations. Leaflets were sought and read with eagerness in an attempt to gain sufficient warning to evacuate the city. Expectation that a bombing of Hanoi would follow immediately after strikes on Mu Gia Pass reportedly caused Hanoi residents to struggle with security police for possession of leaflets. [148/]

SEARCH AND RESCUE

Few Air Force activities could match the drama and human interest of the 3d Aerospace Rescue and Recovery Group (ARRG), the parent organization of the "Jolly Green Giants." The 3d ARRG was activated on 8 January 1966, after a reorganization of SAR forces in SEA was undertaken to establish more effective command and control. The 3d ARRG was assigned to the Pacific Aerospace Rescue and Recovery Center of the Aerospace Rescue and Recovery Service (MAC) and came under operational control of the Commander, 7AF. The Group had a joint Search and Rescue Center, two Rescue Coordination Centers, and two squadrons--the 37th ARRS, Udorn and 38th ARRS, Tan Son Nhut. 149/

The Joint Search and Rescue Center (JSARC) was responsible for coordinating and controlling rescue missions both in-and out-country. In addition, it helped locate overdue aircraft, coordinated intercept for distressed aircraft, provided assistance for medical evacuation and local base rescue efforts. 150/

To accomplish the combat rescue mission, the 3d ARRG staged HH-3 helicopters from Udorn, at forward operating locations/bases so as to be immediately available should an aircraft go down. The HC-130 control aircraft from Udorn flew daylight orbit over Laos, carrying an Airborne Mission Commander (AMC), who was prepared to assume control over the Search and Rescue Task Force when it was launched by the JSARC. The HU-16s from Da Nang flew daylight orbit off the coast of North Vietnam. They would land

PARARESCUE CREW MEMBER checks out forest penetrator
Figure 12

(sea conditions permitting) and recover downed airmen, or remain over their position, while the AMC coordinated the recovery by other means. Aircrews from HH-3E helicopters at Da Nang, or those from the forward operating locations, stood by for rapid reaction to search and rescue missions as directed by JSARC. Whenever possible, the HH-3Es (nicknamed the Jolly Green Giants) were launched in pairs for mutual support. Their reaction speed was approximately 100 knots, endurance 4½ - 5½ hours, and they were equipped with some armor plating, and a hoist with a forest penetrator. 151/

In his trip report of 7 June 1966, Dr. John S. Foster, Jr., Office of the Director of Defense Research and Engineering, stated that the following characteristics were urgently needed in the Jolly Green Giants: 152/

1. Much more speed in transit.

2. Somewhat greater range than the CH-3Cs, although they currently had forward refueling points which helped in this regard.

3. Better night navigation capability, probably best solved by the addition of LORAN D.

4. Night vision devices to permit search for the pilot after dark.

5. More defensive armoring of critical parts, and more armament for fending off capture parties.

Dr. Foster indicated his awareness of Air Force intentions to buy a small number of faster helicopters to augment the Jolly Greens within the next year. He was also cognizant of a joint Navy/Air Force effort to establish a requirement for a new SAR vehicle, however, this might require several years. In the interim, he was anxious to have a more rapid investigation conducted of available means to improve the reaction times of the SAR forces.[153]

During missions, Jolly Green Giants were protected en route and over the rescue site by A-1E aircraft. In the role of escort (RESCORT), A-1Es located survivors and determined the best routes for the helicopter to approach the survivors. They also took measures to discourage hostile forces from interfering with the rescue effort. The excellent coordination between rescue helicopters and their A-1E RESCORT resulted in a highly efficient team, enabling combat rescues to be made under extremely adverse conditions.[154]

Immediately upon receiving a Mayday transmission, tactical support units were launched or diverted to the area to make initial contact with the downed pilot and protect him. The task force was then augmented with fighter, FAC, tanker, ECM, Jolly Green Giants, etc. This small armada was controlled by the JSARC and rescue coordination centers through the AMC. The size of the SAR force was determined by the number and type of aircraft or surface vessel available, that was suitable and necessary for the pickup. The helicopter was the limiting factor in getting to and from the scene. Distance, terrain, and hostile fire, coupled with the vulnerability of the slow, low-flying helicopter, precluded pickup in certain areas. For instance, a 45-degree area bordered by the Red River and the rail lines north to China, and the area within a 30-mile radius of Hanoi, were generally considered inaccessible for rescue forces. If a pilot were downed in the Gulf, at least five miles offshore, however, his chances of rescue were better. Deep in enemy territory, it might take up to two hours for rescue forces to reach the scene. Because of limited night rescue capability, especially in a hostile environment, rescue pickup was usually delayed until daybreak.[155/] There were no "typical" rescue missions since each had unique features and problems. (See Project CHECO Study, "USAF SAR in SEA-1961-1966," 24 Oct 66.)[156/]

Rescue aircraft also performed emergency medical evacuations when directed by proper authority. The U.S. Army was usually able to air evacuate its own wounded from combat areas; however, rescue helicopters frequently were required to evacuate wounded soldiers from areas inaccessible to Army helicopters.[157/]

In addition, HH-43 helicopters of the 3d ARRG were located at 12 air bases in SEA, that had tactical aircraft to provide crash rescue and aircraft fire suppression within close proximity of the base. Some of the HH-43s were configured with self-sealing tanks, auxiliary fuel tanks, and armor plating. This gave them a combat rescue capability, in addition to their local base rescue function.[158/]

The following data reflects the activities of the 3d ARRG during 1966:[159/]

	In-Country	Out-Country
Missions	270	288
Med Evac	134	32
SAR	136	250
Sorties	1,097	952
Combat Saves	239	173
Non-Combat Saves	31	49

On 17 September 1966, a Joint Personnel Recovery Center (JPRC) was activated for the purpose of establishing a capability within MACV, for personnel recovery operations subsequent to termination of sea-air rescue efforts. It served as the coordination authority and focal point for all post-SAR recovery matters in RVN, NVN, Laos, Cambodia, and Thailand. 160/

CHAPTER VI

CONCLUSIONS

Assessment

COMUSMACV concluded that by mid-1966, the enemy could not feel safe in any base area in South Vietnam. Subject to attack by all services of the United States, he could be hit by ground forces, the B-52s, tactical air, and naval gunfire. The forward deployment strategy in the Highlands by midyear had forestalled any major Viet Cong/NVA offensive in that area. According to COMUSMACV, it had been responsible for the decimation of enemy formations in such friendly operations as HAWTHORNE and PAUL REVERE. Not only had the duration of friendly field operations increased, but their spoiling attacks in the II and III CTZs had thrown the Viet Cong off-balance. Friendly operations, such as EL PASO in the III CTZ, north of Saigon, had denied the enemy an opportunity to assemble sufficient forces to win any significant engagements or to sustain a monsoon offensive. [1]

Another significant measure of progress that COMUSMACV noted by midyear was the improved capability of the US/FWMAF and RVNAF to respond rapidly to the Viet Cong/NVA initiatives that had been occurring throughout South Vietnam. He observed that the friendly forces repeatedly had demonstrated their ability to strike rapidly. Especially significant was the fact that these strikes by the friendly forces were in coordinated operations. Equally important, they were being carried out on short notice, and were being conducted effectively with the timely employment of tactical air support.

COMUSMACV said that the overall war effort continued to be increased and improved because of the coordination and cooperation of the RVNAF and the US/FWMA forces. As a good example of this coordination and cooperation, he pointed out an action that took place on 29 June. On that day, the 2d Vietnamese Marine Battalion was moving in convoy on Highway One in the I CTZ. While en route, they came under heavy attack of an estimated enemy battalion.

The VN Marines sent a message reporting the engagement--it was monitored by the U.S. 4th Marines. They notified the Vietnamese forces that the U.S. 4th Marine Artillery would provide fire support; accordingly, these missions were fired as requested. Tactical air strikes were also conducted against the enemy by U.S. and VNAF aircraft; and U.S. Marines and an ARVN airborne battalion were airlifted into the area of operation. Significant about this combined air and ground reaction was its execution in only a matter of hours. As a result of the quick reaction of air support, what was initially a successful Viet Cong ambush, became a costly defeat for the enemy. The Viet Cong, instead of enjoying frequent successes with their ambush tactics, were now encountering severe defeats as a result of the coordinated air and ground actions. 2/

COMUSMACV also told CINCPAC that there were no indications that the enemy resolve had diminished. One point of concern was that the enemy, in fact, was increasing his infiltration. Of significance, was evidence that enemy strength had reached a level from which they could form division-sized units. Still able to maintain his LOCs in South Vietnam, despite heavy air attacks, the enemy also introduced new weapons into his ranks.

With the approach of fall, came increased use of Cambodia, as a safe haven, or for the purpose of moving division-sized forces through the DMZ. COMUSMACV observed that this evidence supported his earlier predictions that the enemy intended to continue a protracted war of attrition. It was important to underline the fact that neither the enemy, nor his determination to continue fighting, should be underestimated. COMUSMACV added that the war could continue to escalate. He felt that infiltration of enemy troops and supplies would continue, offering CINCPAC no assurance that this would not occur. 3/

During the latter part of 1966, it became increasingly evident that the enemy was especially vulnerable to air attack. His long logistics lines of communications were susceptible to interdiction. His logistical base areas could be singled out for destruction. Increased tactical air and the B-52 strikes had wrested from the enemy much of the initiative he had once enjoyed. 4/ By the end of October, CINCPAC told the JCS that air operations in NVN had prevented the enemy from supporting his forces sufficiently to mount any major offensive action, or to seize and hold any vital areas in South Vietnam. He said: "The air campaign was the one action that brought the war home to NVN." He indicated that airstrikes had disrupted the daily life of NVN, and caused multiple and increased management and logistic problems. He concluded that they prevented the enemy from conducting aggression from the comfort of a sanctuary. 5/

COMUSMACV reported that during 1966, the enemy had been hurt in many of these areas. In his principal concentrations near sanctuaries at the DMZ, in the Chu Pong region, and in the Tay Ninh and Binh Long areas, the enemy had suffered heavy losses and had been contained by friendly preemptive operations. At the end of the year, the enemy was avoiding major contact, fighting defensively when forced to do so, and attempting to rebuild and reinforce for winter-spring operations. 6/

Despite his increased vulnerabilities to airstrikes, however, the enemy kept up the fight. A change in the enemy's military strategy reflected this during 1966. It encompassed the new positioning of major North Vietnamese Army (NVA) units in the DMZ, and along the western border areas of central Vietnam. The enemy also massed units of at least regimental strength on several occasions, but when he was engaged in large numbers, he was decisively beaten. Furthermore, the NVA troops took over a major share of the main force mission in I and II Corps area, and the flow of manpower from the Delta was reduced, so as to provide guerrilla replacements in VC main force units of the Delta. 7/

The total enemy force increased from about 251,000 in January 1966, to approximately 280,600 at the end of the year. The total number of enemy battalions, including VC and NVA, increased from about 143 to an estimated 186 during the same period. The number of VC battalions decreased by seven and the NVA increased by 50 battalions. A preponderance of the increase in NVA battalions was in the number (34) of infantry battalions. It was estimated that there were 146 infantry battalions committed at the end of December (65 NVA and 81 VC).[8] By the end of the year, the enemy, despite known losses, had been able to achieve a counter-buildup proportional to the growth of US/FWMA forces. The sources of this increase were in-country conscription and infiltration of personnel from NVN through Laos, Cambodia, and the DMZ.[9]

One of the most notable changes included an increase in antiaircraft fires. The enemy continued to attack airfields occasionally. Infiltration of men and materiel continued and the enemy amassed large stores of war supplies and foodstuffs in base areas, as evidenced by the vast stores captured or destroyed by friendly operations during 1966.[10]

Dedicated, seasoned leadership had been the backbone of the enemy's will to fight in 1966. There was no evidence of any significant lowering of enemy leadership qualities. There had not been an important number of defections among cadre of platoon-level or above. Moreover there was little evidence of less effective operational planning, or control of troops on the battlefield.[11]

Interrogation of enemy captives and returnees indicated that morale had been lowered, due to the effects of airstrikes, personal hardships, the prolonged conflict, inadequate rice, inadequate medicine, and malaria. In addition the North Vietnamese soldiers had suffered the additional hardships of long marches, separation from their families, and disillusionment that the battle was not almost won as had been portrayed to them in NVN. In spite of these indications of the lowering of morale, however, there had not been any appreciable rise in military defections during a six-month period up to mid-October. 12/

The enemy had established and was using an efficient logistics system in South Vietnam during 1966. Moreover, he had disposed his maneuver battalions to take full advantage of his lines of communication and base areas. The enemy continued to have the advantage of fighting from a widely disposed network of supply bases, which were connected by numerous trails and waterways. Ground and air operations against the enemy's base areas had eroded his stocks and were complicating his distribution. The significant point, however, was that few prisoners had complained of a lack of ammunition. 13/

The air campaign directed against NVN was an essential element of U.S. strategy in 1966, for achieving objectives in SEA. Self-imposed controls on the use of airpower against NVN had an adverse impact upon the effectiveness of airpower in reducing the capability of NVN to direct and support the insurgency in SVN. These operations, nevertheless, had a significant impact upon the military capabilities of the NVN Army and the VC. The amount of disruption and enemy materiel destroyed had been of such magnitude as to represent the probable balance of power, which to date had denied the enemy a capability for seizing significant portions of I and II Corps. The enemy had been unable to move concentrations of requisite military force to SVN to accomplish such a task, without incurring unacceptable losses from air attack.[14]

The tactics of the enemy, the nature of the terrain in SVN, and the concealment which was afforded all, dictated that friendly forces must not withhold airpower until the enemy closed in ground combat. CINCPAC stated:[15]

> "We must begin disruption, harassment and attrition of enemy forces as far back as we can find and attack them, thus degrading his capability qualitatively and quantitatively before he reaches the battlefield. Otherwise, his full capability must be met on the battlefield in a mode of combat which is certain to increase our casualties by appreciable and unnecessary numbers."

A standdown of air operations against enemy forces in or within supporting distance of the DMZ, for even the shortest period of time, would create the gravest of risks to the security of friendly forces in the area. The enemy would be accorded a greater freedom of movement for his men and supplies. CINCPAC said, "We cannot afford to risk creation of a sanctuary of this nature close to our own forces."[16]

The air campaign in the north was a major military activity, wherein the U.S. had the initiative and control over the intensity of combat. In SVN, the enemy could engage or disengage on the ground almost at will, thus in a sense pacing the ground war to his advantage. Such was not the case in the air over NVN, where the enemy had to make a concession, if he were to gain any relief from the pressures being applied against him.[17]

There were very serious military risks attached to any form of a partial standdown, either in terms of reducing the targeting base, or in restricting air operations to small geographic areas. As soon as such reductions had become apparent in the past, the enemy had reacted quickly by readjusting his air defenses, and the aircraft attrition rate was increased proportionately. CINCPAC considered it essential that any voluntary simplification or reduction of the enemy's air defense problems should be avoided. In fact, it had become critically apparent from current attrition trends that a broader target base in NVN was urgently needed. [18]

Air operations in NVN had not yet reduced NVN support of the insurgency in SVN to the level desired. Hanoi had not been brought to the negotiating table. Air operations in NVN, however, had prevented the enemy from supporting his forces sufficiently to mount any major offensives, or to seize and hold any vital areas in SVN. The NVN air campaign was the one action that brought the war home to them. It disrupted daily life, and caused multiple and increasing management and logistics problems. It prevented the enemy from conducting an aggression from the comfort of a sanctuary. [19]

In his End of Tour Report, the Deputy Commander, 7AF, commented on the results of the overall USAF efforts in SEA: [20]

> "...I am thoroughly convinced after participating in the planning and execution of combat operations in three wars, that Air Force operations in Vietnam were accomplished more efficiently than any war in the past.
>
> "We have fought this war with the most experienced pilots and professional airmen the Air Force has ever sent into combat. The results which have been achieved are truly outstanding.

"In my judgment, the war in South Vietnam has taken a significant turn for the better during the past year. The large commitment of American forces, both in the air and on the ground, has permitted us to take the initiative away from the enemy. He can no longer mass his forces in selected areas and launch an attack of his own timing. The enemy's operations are inherently time consuming, and with our improved intelligence, we can launch spoiling attacks before he is in position to carry out his plans. With our superior firepower, air mobility of our ground forces and large scale air support, there is no possible way the enemy can hope to achieve any significant military success. There is a great deal of evidence available from captured documents and POW interrogations to confirm low enemy morale and widespread shortages of both food and medical supplies. These facts, plus heavy losses being inflicted by ground and air attacks, could well mean complete disintegration of his combat forces at any time...."

Rand Corporation Appraisal

The Rand Corporation, at the end of 1966, prepared an appraisal of the economic, political, and military effects of the bombing of North Vietnam. Rand summarized that even from the start of the U.S. air offensive against North Vietnam, the Hanoi government appeared to have taken actions to prepare the country for unrestricted air attack, possible ground invasion, and a war of indefinite duration. Rand noted that this effort, combined with effects of the bombing, had imposed a severe strain on North Vietnam's physical and organizational resources. It appeared that the most tangible manifestation of this strain had been a massive diversion of manpower to military and other war-related unproductive activities. Rand observed that the inroads on the agricultural labor force had been particularly serious. In the appraisal, however, he pointed out the following considerations:[21]

"...There is, however, no evidence of critical or progressive deterioration or disruption of economic activity. This reflects that Hanoi has reaped substantial benefits from its response to what, up to mid-1966 at least, was an exaggerated threat assessment. Much of the demand on resources generated by the war effort amounted to investment activity--civil defense, AA defense infrastructure, military mobilization--which, once completed, generates relatively low-cost and sustained benefits. There has also been a large and valuable investment in learning practice, and experience in coping with the tasks and problems imposed by war; a process that was assisted by the specialized and repetitive nature of the U.S. air offensive. Further, Hanoi succeeded in attracting increasing military and economic aid from its allies, China, as well as the USSR, and retained access to these imports. Finally, and apparently on an increased scale in recent months, Hanoi has carried out a large program of evacuation and dispersal of urban population, industrial equipment and--to some unknown extent--administrative agencies.

"The bombing specifically has probably produced enough incidental damage and civilian casualties to assist the government in maintaining anti-American militancy, and not enough to be seriously depressing or disaffecting.

"In short, there is no evidence at present that economically and politically Hanoi should not be able to withstand the long, hard war it professes to have in mind...."

Rand noted that the direct and primary objectives of the air campaign against NVN and Laos were to reduce the level of infiltration, and substantially increase the cost of infiltration of men and equipment from the North to the South. Although the bombing in North Vietnam and Laos did raise the cost of infiltration, Rand observed that the level of infiltration had not been reduced sufficiently during 1966, to prevent North Vietnam from helping to maintain a VC-PAVN combat force in the South, strong enough to deny the prospect of a decisive military victory to the United States and its allies during the year. [22/]

Summary of Results for 1966

The magnitude of air operations in Southeast Asia was vastly increased in 1966. A composite sortie rate of 225,000 per month was being flown in the SEA area of operations throughout the year. This composite rate represented combined sorties of all the services and all the indigenous air forces, including helicopter sorties, but excluding the Military Airlift Command traffic and commercial carriers operating in and out of bases which supported military operations. 23/

During the year, most major indexes used to analyze and evaluate trends increased in favor of friendly forces. USAF aircraft (excluding the B-52 strikes) flew a total of 146,976 attack sorties during 1966 in NVN, Laos, and SVN, and expended 194,820 tons of munitions for this effort. Of the total sorties flown in 1966, 44,494 strike sorties were carried out in NVN to drop 70,017 tons of ordnance. In Laos, there were 32,115 attack sorties which dropped 45,709 tons of munitions. In South Vietnam, in the 70,367 attack sorties, 79,094 tons of munitions were dropped. The ARC LIGHT program, during the year, had conducted 5,332 strike missions, dropping a total of 100,074 tons of munitions in South Vietnam, Laos, North Vietnam, and the DMZ. 24/

In the ROLLING THUNDER program, USAF forces during 1966 conducted 53,533 combat sorties (including recon, ECM, Elint, etc.), with an average munitions expenditure of 1.23 tons per sortie. Strikes in the ROLLING THUNDER area accounted for 62 percent of the total out-country sorties flown. 25/

In Laos, the bulk of the air activity was concentrated in the STEEL TIGER/TIGER HOUND areas. Approximately 79 percent of the 32,672 Air Force combat sorties in Laos were executed in STEEL TIGER/TIGER HOUND, and 21 percent in BARREL ROLL. [26/] By the end of December, combined USAF, USN, and USMC air had expended 76,459.2 tons of munitions in Laos, 77 percent of them being delivered by USAF aircraft. [27/]

Total out-country results achieved by the Air Force through December 1966, were 1,104 bridges destroyed, 1,840 damaged; 6,739 structures destroyed, 4,987 damaged; 2,627 vehicles destroyed, 2,573 damaged; 366 items of railroad equipment destroyed and 437 damaged; and 1,185 watercraft destroyed; 1,535 damaged. Moreover, 9,329 road and railway cuts were made; and 44 ferry slips were destroyed and 177 damaged. A total of 870 AA, SAM, and radar sites were destroyed and 483 were damaged. In addition, an intensive campaign was conducted against POL supplies. This campaign was highlighted by the mass raid in the Hanoi/Haiphong areas on 29 June, in which an estimated 35-45 percent of the NVN POL supplies were destroyed. There were 23 MIG kills during the year. In TIGER HOUND alone, by midyear, U.S. air had accounted for 923 vehicles destroyed, 559 damaged; 128 bridges destroyed, 149 damaged; 175 AAA positions destroyed, 78 damaged; 3,285 structures destroyed; and 1,554 secondary explosions observed. [28/]

During 1966, the Air Force flew 70,578 combat sorties in support of the in-country war, during which 78,716 tons of munitions were expended. The average munitions per sortie for the year was 1.12 tons. The peak activity in air operations in South Vietnam occurred in December, when 7,832 combat sorties were flown and 9,763 tons of munitions were expended. The Air Force flew 52 percent of the total 135,289 combat sorties of U.S. aircraft in SVN.[29]

Airpower in 1966 demonstrated that it could be highly effective throughout RVN, in support of ground actions and mobile operations. This was evidenced by the powerful strikes made against long-held enemy strongholds, troop concentrations, and storage areas in South Vietnam.[30]

Two indexes of progress in-country were the number of enemy killed and the weapons captured. During 1966, approximately 57,510 enemy were killed, with a resultant kill-ratio of 3.51 in favor of friendly forces. The 1965 ratio had been 2.91 with about 36,924 enemy killed.[31]

The Future

At the end of the year, it was concluded that the enemy would continue to carry out the type of operations conducted in 1966. According to predictions, the enemy's strategy during 1967 would include a combination of guerrilla and conventional warfare, with stress on the defensive types of operations.[32]

There was no credible evidence at the end of the year that the communists were considering negotiations to settle the conflict. Their position remained the same--a settlement that included: (1) As outlined in the Geneva Accords, North and South Vietnam had to be unified;

(2) Pending reunification, the provisions of the Geneva agreements had to be respected; (3) Acts of war against North Vietnam had to be stopped and all U.S. troops had to be withdrawn from the RVN; and (4) The South Vietnamese would settle their internal affairs by themselves. 33/

There was no indication that the enemy would revert exclusively to guerrilla warfare. It appeared that the VC/NVA leadership did not consider the situation at the end of the year as sufficiently critical to take such a drastic step on a country-wide basis. Captured documents had indicated a need for increasing guerrilla warfare, but only as a supplement and in conjunction with mobile warfare. With the exception of the IV CTZ, there was no evidence at the end of the year that the VC/NVA forces were thinking of operating in company-size or smaller units. In fact, most of the evidence by the beginning of 1967, indicated that the enemy was moving toward the creation of new and larger units. The trend toward larger units was supported by the fact that, during the last half of 1966, the enemy had formed two divisions in the II and III CTZs. This evidence was supported by the indication that the NVA also were organizing division support and combat support battalions for the various division headquarters, and were infiltrating troops and upgrading Viet Cong units to conventional units. This all appeared to portend that Hanoi probably would attempt to prosecute a protracted war designed to exact maximum attrition of FWMAF under conditions as favorable as possible for the communists. 36/

While the VC/NVA had not launched a major attack since March 1966, there was some evidence at the end of the year, that the VC/NVA were preparing to launch continual and massive conventional-type attacks in widespread areas of the RVN. This evidence included the disposition of enemy forces in the 1st, 2d, and 3d CTZs, the continuing formation of division-size units from separate regiments and infiltrated NVA units, the creation of senior headquarters, the increased use of mortars and artillery, and the stockpiling of all classes of military supplies. Propaganda statements, agent reports, POW statements, and captured documents all portend this trend.

Significant factors, however, were in evidence at the end of the year, that the enemy would not utilize his capability of launching massive and continual conventional-type attacks in 1967. Important factors which might negate the enemy's attempting to utilize this capability were the "spoiling attacks" in 1966. These attacks had preempted the initiative and prevented the enemy from launching his offensive.

Another factor, the increased level of combat, would place a heavy strain on the enemy's tenuous supply system. It appeared doubtful that enemy LOCs, existing at the end of the year, could provide a continuous supply, such as would be required for these operations. Heavy tonnage items (artillery and mortar ammunitions) would also have to be stockpiled far in advance. Such action probably would not be taken by the enemy, since it would reduce his tactical flexibility and probably tip off a pending offensive. 35/

In conclusion, it was believed that the VC/NVA would continue to maintain in 1967, his large Main Force units. Additionally, the enemy would continue to maintain a logistical base in the RVN, in North Vietnam, near and in the DMZ, and in Laos that was capable of sustaining his forces. It was believed also that the enemy's out-of-country logistical support would give priority to those VC/NVA forces operating in the 1st CTZ and the Highland areas. It was felt that in the 1st, 2d, and 3d CTZs, the enemy would attempt in 1967, to draw FWMAF units into pitched battles under conditions favorable to him in order to inflict major losses upon the FWMAF. In 1967, also, the enemy might shift and group his forces, so as to pose significant threats throughout the RVN and especially in the 1st, 2d, and 3d CTZs. While it was believed that the VC/NVA were fully aware of the vulnerability of their massing forces to friendly air, ground, and naval firepower, it was felt that the enemy would be willing in 1967, to accept heavy losses in an engagement, if he were confident that he could inflict heavy losses upon friendly forces. [36]

By the end of 1966, the enemy appeared to have reached an impasse in the conflict. One big problem that would face him in 1967, was the necessity of increasing infiltrator and recruit inputs to match the battle losses, the deserters, and the non-battle casualties which had shown an ever-increasing trend. [37]

Communist Chinese Intentions

While North Vietnam had announced on 9 November 1966, that ethnic Chinese living in North Vietnam were flocking to volunteer to join the

NVA, evidence did not indicate that "volunteer" troops would be introduced into the RVN in the immediate future. Should foreign volunteers be introduced, the most likely would be Chinese troops wearing NVA uniforms, which probably would be integrated into the NVA units. [38]

The Communist Chinese, however, did have the capability to intervene in the Vietnam war, and by the end of 1966, there were indications that they had a readiness posture to do so. By the beginning of 1967, the Communist Chinese military forces were in a high state of readiness, and an advanced logistical theater command had been established in North Vietnam. Indicators in the political and economic areas, however, did not point as strongly toward intervention. Aside from logistical support, there was no credible evidence of the Vietnamese' desire for Communist Chinese military assistance in the RVN. [39]

FOOTNOTES

CHAPTER I

1. (U) Review of 1966, Gen. W. C. Westmoreland; Supplement to Policy Letter for Commander, Office of the Secretary of the Air Force, Jan 67.

2. (U) American Security Council Report, 2 Jan 66;
   (U) Ltr, Ho Chi Minh to Heads of State, 28 Jan 66, New York Times, 1 Feb 66.
   (C) Embtel, Saigon 4-1071-A, 9 Apr 66;
   (S) Fact Sheet, President's Asian Trip, subj: Negotiating Positions of the DRV and NLFSV, 10 Oct 66.

3. Ibid.

4. (S) Briefing for SECDEF, MACVJ-2 Brig. Gen. McChristian, 10 Oct 66.

5. Ibid.

6. Ibid.

7. (TS) Msg, 2AD, AFSSO, to PACAF, AFSSO, 030925, AF Eyes Only, Dec 65.

8. Ibid.

9. (TS) Msg, CINCPAC to COMUSMACV and Others, 120430Z Jan 66.

10. (TS) Honolulu Planning Conference CY 66 Capabilities Program, Vol. I, Jan 66.

11. Ibid.

12. Ibid.

13. Ibid.

14. Ibid.

15. Ibid.

16. (TS) Msg, CINCPAC, 052050Z Sep 66.

17. (S) Memo, 7AF, subj: List of 7AF OPLANS/OPORDS, 18 Dec 66.

FOOTNOTES

CHAPTER II

1. (U) Memo, 7AF Comdr to Dep Comdr, 7/13 AF and Others, subj: Rules of Engagement for Southeast Asia;
   (TS) DPLP-AD, 7 Sep 66.

2. <u>Ibid</u>.

3. <u>Ibid</u>.

4. <u>Ibid</u>.

5. <u>Ibid</u>.

6. (U) Memo, 7AF Comdr to Dep Comdr, 7/13AF and Others, subj: Rules of Engagement for SEA;
   (TS) DPLD-AD, 7 Sep 66.

7. <u>Ibid</u>.

8. <u>Ibid</u>.

9. (TS) DPLD-AD, 7 Sep 66.

10. <u>Ibid</u>.

11. <u>Ibid</u>.

12. <u>Ibid</u>.

13. (TS) Msg, CINCPAC, 272336Z Jul 66.

14. (TS) Msg, CINCPAC to JCS and Others, subj: Rules of Engagement for Vietnam DMZ, 180833Z Jul 66.

15. (TS) Msg, CINCPAC, 272336Z, Jul 66; Msg, JCS, 302123Z Jul 66.

16. (TS) Msg, COMUSMACV, 061215Z, Aug 66.

17. (U) Memo, 7AF Comdr, to Dep Comdr, 7/13AF and Others, subj: Rules of Engagement for SEA, no date.
    (TS) DPLP-AD, 7 Sep 66.

18. (TS) Command History, USMACV, 1966.

19. (U)   Memo from 7AF Commander to Dep Comdr, 7/13AF and Others, subj: Rules of Engagement for SEA;
    (TS) DPLP-AD, 7 Sep 66.

20. (TS) DPLP-AD, 7 Sep 66.

21. (TS) Msg, COMUSMACV to DCG, USARV, 231148 Dec 66.

22. (S)   Msg, CINCPAC to COMUSMACV, 252240Z, Dec 65; Embtel, Bangkok, to 2AD, 230550Z, Dec 65; Msg, CINCPAC to COMUSMACV, 252240Z, Dec 65.

23. (TS) Msg, 2AD to CINCPAC, 090248Z Feb 66.

24.   Ibid.

25. (TS) Msg, AMEMB Bangkok, to 2AD, 230550Z, Dec 65;
    (TS) Msg, AMEMB Vientiane, to SECSTATE, 061036Z, Jan 66;
    (TS) Msg, AMEMB Vientiane to COMUSMACV, 301100Z, Mar 66;
    (TS) Msg, AMEMB Vientiane to COMUSMACV, 060958Z, Apr 66.

26. (TS) Msg, USAIRA, Vientiane, to COMUSMACV, 310127Z, Dec 65;
    (TS) Msg, COMUSMACV to CINCPAC, MAC 0270, 12 Jan 66.

27. (TS) Msg, SECSTATE, 240023Z, Mar 66; Embtel, Vientiane, 251215Z, Mar 66; OPRD 433-66, DOCO 03878, 270610Z Nov 65; Embtel, Vientiane, to COMUSMACV, 301100Z, Mar 66.

28. (TS) USAIRA, Vientiane, to 7AF, 01231, 270822Z Jul 66.

29. (TS) End of Tour Rpt, Maj. Gen. Gilbert L. Meyers, Dep Comdr, 2AD and 7AF, 23 Apr 65 - 1 Aug 66.

30. (S)   Msg, 2AD to ALLCOM, 022105Z Feb 66.

31. (TS) Msg, CINCPAC, subj: ROLLING THUNDER, 020255Z Apr 66.

32. (TS) Msg, CINCPAC, 160922 Jun 66; Msg, JCS to CINCPAC, 222044Z Jun 66.

33. (TS) Briefing for Wesley Melyan, Project CHECO, by Lt. Cornell, USN, Apr 67.

34.   Ibid.

35.   Ibid.

36. (TS) Msg, JCS to CINCPAC, 3213/301210, Jun 66.

37.   Ibid.

38.   Ibid.

39.   Ibid.

40.   Ibid.

41. (S)   Msg, Hq 7AF to Subordinate Cmds, 020930Z, Apr 66.

42. (TS)   Msg, 2AD to CSAF, 05564, 251246Z, Mar 66.

43. (TS)   Msg, 630 CSO TUOC Udorn, Thailand, to 7AF TS TUOC, 01355, 250806Z, May 66.

44.   Ibid.

45. (TS)   Msg, 35 TFW, Da Nang AB to 7AF TS LIMDIS, 35 DO, TSC-66-4796, 230215Z May 66;
    (S)   Msg, 7AF, FASTEL, 12 May 66.

46. (TS)   Msg, 7AF to 630 CSG, Udorn AB, Thailand, and others, LIMDIS, DOCO-EE-TS-10326/091028Z, Jun 66.

47. (TS)   Msg, 7AF to Hq USAF and PACAF, TS, FASTEL/DOCO-E-TS-129, 180715Z, 18 Jun 66.

48.   Ibid.

49. (S)   Rpt, 7AF, Highlights, 1966,

50.   Ibid.

51.   Ibid.

52.   Ibid.

53.   Ibid.

54. (TS)   Msg, CINCPACAF to 7AF, TS, DO 30 439, 070222Z, 7 Oct 66.

55. (S)   Rpt, Summary of Effects of Air Operations, DI, PACAF, Jan 66.

56.   Ibid.

57.   Ibid.

58.   Ibid.

59. (TS)   Msg, CINCPAC to JCS, 041658 Jan 66.

60. (TS)   Msg, CINCPAC to CJCS, 240215Z Jan 66.

61. (TS) Msg, COMUSMACV to CG, III MAF and Others, 03003, 300415Z Jan 66.

62. (TS) Msg, CINCPAC to COMUSMACV, 060736 Jan 66.

63. (TS) Msg, CINCPAC to COMUSMACV, 060736 Jan 66.

64. Ibid.

65. Ibid.

66. Ibid.

67. (TS) Msg, CINCPAC to COMUSMACV, 092122Z Jan 66.

68. (TS) Msg, COMUSMACV to CINCPAC, 01174, 130120Z Jan 66.

69. (TS) Msg, COMUSMACV to CINCPAC, 01363, 141236Z Jan 66.

70. (TS) Msg, CINCPAC to JCS, 152032Z Jan 66.

71. Ibid.

72. (TS) CINCPAC to JCS, 152032Z, Jan 66;
    (TS) CINCPAC to COMUSMACV, 192340, Jan 66.

73. (C) Msg, SECDEF to COMUSMACV, 2117, 202253 Jan 66.

74. (U) Chronology, 7AF, 1 Jul 65-30 Jun 66.

75. (C) Msg, COMUSMACV to CINCPAC, 02631, 261449Z Jan 66.

76. (TS) Msg, COMUSMACV, MACCOC, 54583, 261240Z Dec 66.

77. (TS) Msg, CINCPAC to CJCS, 290647Z, Dec 66.

78. (TS) Msg, CINCPAC to COMUSMACV, 290647Z Dec 66.

79. (TS) Msg, COMUSMACV to CINCPAC, 021430Z, Jan 67.

80. (TS) Summary Air Operations Southeast Asia, Vol XIV, Hq PACAF, AF EYES ONLY, 24 Dec 65-6 Jan 66.

81. (TS) Msg 7AF to ALCON, 290936Z Dec 66.

82. (TS) Msg, CINCPACAF to 2AD, LIMDIS 50004, 120100Z Jan 66.

83. (TS) Ltr, Hq USAF, (C) Peacetime Conduct of USAF Military Personnel Who are Lost, Detained or Otherwise Isolated in Areas Controlled by USSR, Communist China or their Satellites, para 4b, dtd 7 May 1959.

84. (TS) Msg, CINCPACAF to 2AD, LIMDIS, 50004, 120100Z, Jan 66.

85. (S)   Msg, CSAF AFXPDO 2125/65 Nov 65, 102121Z Nov 65;
          Msg, CSAF AFPTRF 1907/65 Oct 65, 062133Z Oct 65.

86. (TS) Msg, CINCPACAF to 2AD LIMDIS 50004, 120100Z Jan 66.

87. (TS) Msg, CINCPACAF to CSAF, LIMDIS 50005, 172230Z Jan 66.

FOOTNOTES

CHAPTER III

1. (TS) Command History USMACV, 1966.

2. (TS) End of Tour Report, Gen. Gilbert L. Myers, Dep Comdr, 7AF, 31 Jul 66.

3. Ibid.

4. Ibid.

5. Ibid.

6. (TS) Msg, 7AF to SAC 18907 Oct 66, AF EYES ONLY, Ref (TS) CINCP 3634 Oct 66, 250112Z Oct 66.

7. (S) Msg, 7AFSSO - 01780, to AFSSO PACAF, SPECAT AF EYES ONLY, subj: B-52 Operations, 6 Oct 66.

8. (TS) Memo for Gen. Moore fm BG G. B. Simler, Hq 7AF DCS/Opns, subj: Command and Control of Air Resources in SEA, 28 Mar 66.

9. (S) Memo MACJ-2 to 2AD Commander and Others, subj: Enhancement to Airstrike Sortie Effectiveness, 26 Jan 66.

10. Ibid.

11. Ibid.

12. (TS) Msg, 7AF to PACAF TS DOPR-OL-08881, 190855Z May 66.

13. Ibid.

14. Ibid.

15. (TS) Memo, 7AF Commander to MACV, subj: Requirement for Contingency Plan, 18 Jun 66.

16. (TS) Memo, Gen Moore fm BG G. B. Simler, DCS/Opns Hq 7AF, 28 Mar 66.

17. (S) End of Tour Report, Director of Intelligence, 7AF 6 Mar 65 - 1 Jul 66.

18. (S) Comdr, 7AF, to AFXPD, USAF 00602, 22 Sep 66.

19. (S)   Correspondence, AFCCS 12-01, Gen McConnell to Gen Momyer, AF EYES ONLY, subj: B-52 ADVON, 1 Nov 66.

20. (C)   Msg, JCS to COMUSMACV, 7AF, CINCPAC and Others, 1918, 211713 Dec 66.

21. (S)   Msg, COMUSMACV to CINCPAC, 54554, 261157Z Dec 66.

22. (S)   Msg, JCS to COMUSMACV and Others, 2981, 061805Z Jan 66.

23. (S)   7AF Highlights, DO, 7AF, PACAF, 1966.

24. (TS) Memo, Gen Moore, fm BG G. B. Simler, DCS/Opns, Hq 7AF, subj: Command and Control of Air Resources in Southeast Asia, 28 Mar 66.

25. (TS) Msg, 2AD AFSSO to PACAF AFSSO, AF EYES ONLY, 05739, subj: Command and Control, 28 Mar 66.

26. (TS) Msg, CINCPACAF to CSAF, AF EYES ONLY, 50501, 062135Z, Sep 66.

27. (TS) Special CHECO Study, "Control of Airstrikes in SEA 1961-1966."

28. (S)   Monthly Air Intelligence Newsletter, Hq 2AD, 12 Mar 66.

FOOTNOTES

CHAPTER IV

1. (S)   Command Status, 7AF, Dec 66.

2. (TS) Command Status, 2AD, Jan 66;
   (S)   Command History, USMACV 1965.

3. (S)   Command Status, 7AF, Dec 66; Annual Supplement, Hq PACAF, Summary, Air Opns SEA, CY 1966.

4. (S)   Command Status, 2AD, Jan 66; Command Status, 7AF, Dec 66.

5. (S)   Msg, COMUSMACV, 070659Z Dec 65.

6. (TS) Msg, CINCPAC, 120744Z Jan 66.

7. (S)   Msg, COMUSMACV to CINCPAC, 230044Z Jan 66.

8. (TS) Document, CINCPAC, CY 66 Capabilities Program, Feb 66.

9.   Ibid.

10. (C) Msg, COMUSMACV, 210849Z Jan 66;
    (S) MONEVAL, MACJ 341, Jan, Feb, Mar 66.

11. (TS) Msg, CINCPAC, 040704Z Apr 66.

12. (TS) Msg, JCS, 7870, 062131Z Apr 66; Msg, JCS, 7870, 062131Z Apr 66; Ref Doc, JCSM-218-66, 4 Apr 66.

13. (TS) Msg, CINCPAC, 200325 Apr 66.

14. (TS) Msg, COMUSMACV, 060608Z May 66; Msg, CINCPAC, 200325Z Apr 66.

15. (TS) Interview, Lt Col K. H. Muse, USAF, MACJ-32 with Lt Col J. C. Stokes, USAF, (MHB), MACJ031, 10 May 66;
    (S) Command Status, Hq 7AF, Apr 66.

16. (TS) Document, USMACV Force Requirements, Honolulu Planning Conference, May - Jun 66.

17.   Ibid.

18.   Ibid.

19. (TS) Msg, CINCPAC to COMUSMACV, 120450Z Aug 66.

20.   Ibid.

21. (TS) Msg, COMUSMACV to 7AF, 300222Z Jul 66; Msg, JCS to CINCPAC, 022138Z Aug 66.

22. (S) Msg, CINCPACAF to CINCPAC, 050422Z Aug 66; Rpt, USMACV Monthly Historical Summary J3, Aug 66; Msg, CINCPAC to CINCPACAF, COMUSMACV, 19 Aug 66; Msg, COMUSMACV to CINCPAC, 161206Z Aug 66.

23. (S) Rpt, USMACV MONEVAL, Aug 66.

24. (TS) Msg, CINCPAC to COMUSMACV, 250011 Dec 66.

25. (S) AFAG-MACV Debriefing Report of BG Albert W. Schinz, Chief, AFAG, 9 Jul 65 - 23 October.

26. (S) Ltr fm COMUSMACV to CINCPAC, 11 Apr 67.

27. (S) Debriefing Report, Chief, AFAG, BG Albert W. Schinz, 9 Jul 65 - 23 Oct 65. (Hereafter cited: BG A. W. Schinz Debriefing.)

28. (TS) Command History, 1966.

29. (S) Command Status, Dec 66, Hq MACV, BG A. W. Schinz Debriefing.

30. (S) MONEVAL, MACJ-341, Aug 66.

31. (TS) Hq MACV Command History, 1966; 7AF Command Status, Dec 66.

32. (S) Ltr COMUSMACV to CINCPAC, 11 Apr 67; Command Status, 7AF, Dec 66;
    (TS) Command History, Hq MACV, 1966; Historical Summary, 7AF, Jun 66.

33. (S) Ltr, COMUSMACV to CINCPAC, 11 Apr 67.

34. (S) Historical Summary, AFAG, May 66.

35. (S) MONEVAL, MACJ, 341, Jul 66; Command Status, 7AF, Dec 66.

36. (S) BG Albert W. Schinz Debriefing.

37. (TS) Command History, MACV, 1966.

38. (TS) Command History, MACV 1966; History of USAF Construction in Vietnam, 7AF (to be published in 1967).
    (U) RVN Airfield Listing, 834th AD, 31 Mar 67.

39. (TS) Command History, MACV 1966.

40. (S) Ltr, 7AF, subj: Significant Events Calendar Year 1966, 2 Feb 67.

41. Ibid.

42. Ibid.

43. (S) Msg, Maj Gen W. E. DePuy to Gen W. C. Westmoreland and Rosson, HWA, 0211, 19 Jan 66.

44. (TS) Msg, CINCPAC to CJCS, 242152Z Apr 66.

45. (TS) Historical Briefing, Gen W. C. Westmoreland, 9 Apr 66.

46. (S) Ltr, 7AF, subj: Significant Events Calendar Year 1966, 2 Feb 67.

47. Ibid.

48. Ibid.

49. Ibid.

50. Ibid.

51. (U) Statement, Hon Harold Brown, SECAF, on "Posture and the FY 1968 Air Force Budget," 2 Feb 66.

52. (TS) Command History, MACV, 1966.

53. (S) Report, PACAF DOTE, Counterinsurgency Lessons Learned, 21 Jun 66.

54. Ibid.

55. Ibid.

56. Ibid.

57. Ibid.

58. (TS) End of Tour Report, 7AF, Dep Comdr, Maj Gen Gilbert L. Meyers, Deputy Commander, 23 Apr 65 - 1 Aug 66.

59. (TS) Msg, COMUSMACV, 06555, 1 Mar 66; DF, MACJ4, 19 Feb 66.

60. (TS) Msg, CINCPAC, 040037Z Feb 66; DF MACJ4, 19 Feb 66;
    (S) Msg, CINCPAC, 050021Z May 66.

61. (S) Msg, COMUSMACV, 06555, 1 Mar 66;
    (TS) DF, MACJ4, 19 Feb 66;
    (TS) Briefing, for DEP SECDEF, 3 Apr 66.

62. (S) Msg, COMUSMACV, MAC, 3092, subj: Ref Telecon and CINCPAC Msg, 100040Z Apr (Back Channel), 18 Apr 66.

63. (TS) Msg, PACAF to 7AF, C30189, 270214Z Apr 66.

64. Ibid.

65. Ibid.

66. (TS) Msg, CJCS to CINCPAC and COMUSMACV, JCS, 1974, 13 Apr 66. Telecon, NMCC to MACV, Taped Interview, 241500Z Apr 66.

67. (TS) Msg, COMUSMACV to CINCPAC, 14250, 251225Z Apr 66.

68. (TS) Msg, PACAF to 7AF, DOP, 30278, 022125Z Jul 66, msg, PACAF to CINCPAC DOP, 30256, 170511Z Jun 66.

69. (TS) Msg, PACAF to 7AF, FASTEL, 038, AFEO, 102358Z Sep 66.

70. (TS) Command History, MACV, 1966.

71. (TS) End of Tour Report, Maj Gen Gilbert L. Meyers, Dep Comdr, 23 Apr 65 - 1 Aug 66.

FOOTNOTES

CHAPTER V

1. (TS)   Summary of SEA Air Operations (Jan - Nov 1966) BG Joseph J. Kruzel, 13 Dec 66.

2. (TS)   Project CHECO Special Report, "TIGER HOUND," 6 Sep 66.

3. (TS)   Msg, COMUSMACV to CINCPAC, 15147, 031024Z May 66; Msg, CINCPAC to COMUSMACV, 23 Aug 66; Msg, COMUSMACV to CINCPAC, 15147, 031024Z May 66.

4. (TS)   Project CHECO Special Report, "TIGER HOUND," 6 Sep 66.

5. (TS)   Msg, COMUSMACV to CINCPAC, 15147, 031024Z May 66.

6. (TS)   Project CHECO Special Report, "TIGER HOUND," 6 Sep 66.

7. (TS)   Project CHECO Special Report, "Air Operations in the DMZ," 15 Feb 67.

8.   Ibid.

9. (TS)   Project CHECO Special Report, "Operation TALLY HO," 21 Nov 66.

10.   Ibid.

11.   Ibid.

12. (TS)   Project CHECO Special Report, "Air Operations in the DMZ," 15 Feb 67.

13.   Ibid.

14.   Ibid.

15.   Ibid.

16. (TS)   Memo, USMACV, MACJ-03, subj: Udorn Conference 10 Mar 66.

17. (TS)   Comdr, 2AD to COMUSMACV, 131106, Mar 66;
    (S)   Msg, COMUSMACV to CINCPAC/Amemb, Vientiane, 261400Z Mar 66.

18. (TS)   Msg, COMUSMACV to CINCPAC 13308, 171110Z Apr 66.

19. (S)   Staff Conf, USMACV, MACJ031, 29 Apr 66.
    (TS)   Msg, COMUSMACV to CINCPAC, 14620, 280943 Apr 66.

20. (S) Msg, 7AF to NMCC and CINCPAC, 18485, 270637Z Apr 66.

21. (TS) Msg, CINCPAC to JCS, 300405Z Apr 66. Msg, COMUSMACV to CINCPAC (MACCOC), 14735, 290745Z Apr 66. Msg, JCS J3 9629, 291503Z Apr 66. Msg, CINCPAC to JCS, 300405Z Apr 66.

22. (U) News Article, U.S. News & World Report, 28 Mar 66.

23. (TS) Honolulu Conference Capabilities Program, Vol I, 1966.

24. (U) News Article, Chicago Tribune, 11 Feb 66.
    (TS) Msg, CINCPAC to CINCPACAF, CINCPACFLT and COMUSMACV 300305Z Jan 66. Summary of Events, MACJ-3, 7-13 Feb 66.

25. (TS) Msg, CINCPAC to COMUSMACV, CINCPACAF, CINCPACFLT, 010200Z Apr 66.

26. (TS) Rpt, Honolulu Requirements Planning Conf, Jun 66.

27. Ibid.

28. (TS) Msg, CINCPAC to JCS 060800Z Jun 66.

29. (TS) Msg, JCS to CINCPAC, 222044Z Jun 66. Summary, Air Opns, SEA, Hq PACAF, Jun 66; Memo, Comdr, 7AF to COMUSMACV, 3 Jul 66.
    (U) News Article, New York Times, 30 Jun 66.

30. (TS) SEA Air Opns, Aug 66.
    (S) MONEVAL, MACJ-341, Aug 66.
    (TS) Msg, CINCPACAF to 7AF 270420Z Sep 66; Msg, CINCPAC to JCS, 261920Z Oct 66.

31. (TS) SEA Air Opns, PACAF, Aug 66.

32. (TS) Msg, CINCPAC to CINCPACFLT, CINCPACAF, COMUSMACV, 310242 Dec 66.

33. Editor's Note.

34. (S) Ltr, 7AF, subj: Significant Events Calendar Year 1966, 2 Feb 67.

35. (TS) Msg, CINCPAC to CINCPACFLT, CINCPACAF, COMUSMACV, 180054Z Sep 66.

36. (TS) Msg, CINCPACAF to CINCPAC, 152045Z Oct 66.

37. (S) Effects of Air Opns SEA, Hq PACAF, 1 Jan-31 Mar 66; WAIS 19 Sep 66.

38. (TS) Msg, AFCP to CINCPACAF, 028330Z Dec 66.

39. (S) Ltr, 7AF, subj: Significant Events CY 1966, 2 Feb 67.

40. Editor's Note.

41. (TS) Msg, CINCPACAF to CINCPAC, 101946 Jan 67.

42. Ibid.

43. Ibid.

44. Msg, JCS to CINCPAC, COMUSMACV, Cite JCC 5586-66, 170047Z Sep 66.

45. (TS) Msg, COMUSMACV to Lt Gen Starbird, MACV 8242, 210742Z Sep 66.

46. (TS) Annex C, Hq USMACV, MACV Practice Nine Requirements Plan, 26 Nov 66.

47. Ibid.

48. Ibid.

49. Ibid.

50. Ibid.

51. Ibid.

52. Ibid.

53. Ibid.

54. Ibid.

55. Msg, COMUSMACV to SECDEF, JCS and CINCPAC, 02051, 210635Z Jan 66.

56. Ibid.

57. Ibid.

58. Ibid.

59. (TS) Msg, CINCPAC to JCS, 922232 Jul 66.

60. (TS) Annex C, Hq USMACV, MACV Practice Nine Requirements Plan, 26 Nov 66.

61. Ibid.

62. (TS) Msg, COMUSMACV to DCPG, Washington, D. C. 271001Z Oct 66.

63. (TS) Msg, COMUSMACV to CINCPAC 190845 Jan 67.

64. (TS) Special Study, Hq MACV, CIC, Research & Analysis, ST 67-003, "Evaluation of Herbicide Operations in RVN," 12 Jul 66.

65. (S) WAIS, 7AF, 11 Jun 66.

66. Ibid.

67. (S) Pink Rose Test Plan, 7AF, 26 Dec 66; Msg, 7AF to CINCPAC 060535Z Apr 67.

68. Ibid.

69. (S) Msg, JCS to CINCPAC, 192352 Dec 66; Msg, CINCPAC to COMUSMACV 292041Z Dec 66.

70. (S) Msg, CINCPAC to PACAF, 282200Z Nov 66.

71. Special Study, Hq MACV, CIC, Research & Analysis, ST 67-003, "Evaluation of Herbicide Operations in RVN," 12 Jul 66.

72. Ibid.

73. Ibid.

74. (S) Msg, COMUSMACV to CINCPAC, 140754Z Dec 66.

75. Ibid.

76. (TS) Msg, CINCPAC to CINCPACAF, 18 Sep 66.

77. (TS) Opns Plan, 7AF, Nr 463-67, 23 Sep 66.

78. (TS) Msg, CINCPAC to CINCPACAF, 18 Sep 66.

79. (TS) Msg, COMUSMACV to CINCPAC, 16 Nov 66.

80. Ltr, 7AF, subj: Significant Events Calendar Year 1966, 2 Feb 67.

81. (U) Statement, CSAF, Gen. John P. McConnell, "Armed Forces Management," Oct 66.

82. (TS) Msg, 2AD to CINCPAC, 090248 Feb 66.

83. Ibid.

84. (S) Ltr, Hq 7AF, subj: Staff Action Items, 3 Jan 67; Ltr DOA to

Hq 7AF, subj: Staff Action Items, 12 Jan 67.

85. (S) Study Group Report JCS, "A Comparative Analysis of AF and USMC CAS Performance in SVN, 19 Feb 66.

86. (C) Msg, COMUSMACV to Comdr IV Advisory Grp, 19 Aug 66. Msg III DASC 27 Aug 66.

87. (S) Msg, III DASC, Operations Analysis, 27 Aug 66, Hq USAF "Effectiveness of Close and Direct Air Support in South Vietnam," Jun 66.

88. (S) Project CHECO Special Report, "Operation MASHER/WHITE WING," 9 Sep 66.

89. (S) Project CHECO Special Report, "The Fall of A Shau," 29 Mar 66.

90. (S) Project CHECO Special Report, Operation HAWTHORNE, 8 Sep 66.

91. (S) Project CHECO Special Report, Operation EL PASO, Oct 66.

92. Ibid.

93. (S) Project CHECO Special Report, "Operation ATTLEBORO," 14 Apr 67.

94. Ibid.

95. (S) MACJ-341, MONEVAL, JACJ-341, Dec 66.

96. (TS) Effects of Air Operations, SEA, PACAF, (DO) Jan-Dec 66.

97. (TS) Study, 7AF, Airstrike Sortie Effectiveness, 6 Feb 66.

98. (S) Special Report, CICV, Effects of B-52 Raids, 8 Apr 66.

99. (S) Msg, 7AF, Comdr to AFXPD, USAF 00602, 22 Sep 66; Memo for Record, Gen Momyer, Command and Control of B-52s, 30 Oct 66.

100. (TS) Project CHECO, Report, "The Expanding Role of B-52 Operations in SEA 1966," AFEO, 1967.

101. Ibid.

102. Ibid.

103. (TS) Msg, CINCPAC to JCS, 160155Z Dec 66; Msg, CINCPAC to CJCS, 230338Z Dec 66.

104. (S) Msg, COMUSMACV to VMAC, 100140Z Dec 66.

105. (S) Msg, CINCPACAF to CINCSAC, 110015Z Feb 67; Ltr MACJ 02 to DEPCOMUSMACV 12 Jan 67.

106. (S) Report, PACAF "Effects of Air Operations SEA," 1 Jan-31 Mar 66.

107. (TS) Msg, COMUSMACV to CINCPAC, 27891, 12 Aug 66;
(S) Special Rpt, CICV, Nr 10, Effects of B-52 Raids, 8 Apr 66.

108. (TS) Commanders Conf, MACV, 20 Nov 66.

109. (TS) Memo, Gen Momyer, 7AF Comdr, to Gen Jones, B-52 Concept, 7 Aug 66.

110. Special Report, DIT, 7AF, "Effectiveness of B-52 Strikes in SEA," 25 Jun 66.

111. (TS) Special Report, PACAF, "Summary of Air Operations," May 1966; End of Tour Report, 7AF, DI, B/Gen Rockly Triantafellu, 6 Mar 65-1 Jul 66.

112. (U) SO G-41, PACAF, 15 Dec 65; SO G-269, PACAF, 8 Sep 66.
(S) Command Status, 2AD, Jan 66.
(TS) CHECO Study, PACAF, "USAF Reconnaissance in SEA," 25 Oct 66; End of Tour Report, Maj James R. Baines, 10 Feb 67.

113. (TS) CHECO Study, PACAF, "USAF Reconnaissance in SEA," 25 Oct 66.

114. (TS) Msg, CINCPACAF, 230356, 24 Aug 66; Special Rpt, PACAF, "Summary Air Opns, SEA," Dec 66.

115. (TS) Briefing, MACVJ-2, for Gen H. K. Johnson, OCFFSA, 30 Jul 66. Msg, SAC to CINCPAC, 262150 Apr 66; Msg, CINCPACFLT to CINCPAC 230437Z Apr 66.

116. Ltr, Hq USAF, subj: Transmitting Briefing for Front End Crew Members (ARDF) "Phyllis Ann,".

117. (TS) CHECO Study, PACAF, USAF Reconnaissance in SEA, 25 Oct 66.

118. (TS) Ltr, Hq USAF, subj: Transmitting Briefing for Front End Crew Members (ARDF) "Phyllis Ann," 22 Apr 66.

119. (TS) Medical Rpt, PACAF, Summary of Air Opns, SEA, Dec 66.

120. Editor's note.

121. (S) Project CHECO Special Study, PACAF, "Assault Airlift Operations," AFEO 23 Feb 67.

122. (C)   Briefing, Comdr, 834th AD to CINCPACAF, 26 Jan 67.
    (SNF) Rpt, 834th AD Management Analysis, Tactical Airlift Performance Analysis, SEA, Dec 66.

123. (C)   Briefing, Comdr, 834th AD to CINCPACAF, 26 Jan 67.

124.   Ibid.

125.   Ibid.

126.   Ibid.

127. (C)   Ibid; Project CHECO Interview, Maj B. A. Whitaker, CHECO, with Col David R. Lewis, 463d Troop Carrier Wing, 14 Nov 66.

128. (S)   Msg, COMUSMACV, 120110Z Oct 66; Msg, CHWTO, WTO 303, 140806Z Oct 66; Msg, CINCPACAF, 52498, 160545Z Oct 66.

129. (S)   Command Correspondence Staff Summary Sheet, DCS/Plans, Col A. L. Hilpert, USAF, 16 Nov 66. (Hereafter cited: Command Correspondence Staff Summary Sheet.)

130. (U)   Joint Basic Plan, "Red Leaf," CV-2/7 Transfer, 8 Jun 66.

131. (S)   Ltr, 7AF, 2 Feb 66, Subj: (U) Significant Events Calendar Year 66.

132.   Ibid.

133. (C)   Commander 834th Air Div Briefing to CINCPACAF, 26 Jan 67.

134. (S)   7AF ltr, 2 Feb 66 subj: Significant Events Calendar Year 66, 2 Feb 67.

135.   Ibid.

136. (S)   Command Correspondence Staff Summary Sheet, 28 Oct 66.

137. (S)   Ltr, 7AF, Vice Comdr, subj: Project Red Leaf, 11 Oct 66.

138. (S)   End of Tour Report, 5th ACS, Sqn Cdr, Lt Col Joseph F. Baier, Jr., 9 Sep 66. (Hereafter cited Baier End of Tour Report.)

139.   Ibid.

140.   Ibid.

141. (S)   Msg, COMUSMACV, Cite 45493, subj: Psychological Opns, 20 Dec 65.

142.   Baier, End of Tour Report.

143. (S) Rpt, Hq USMACV, MACJ5, Analysis of MACV Psywar Posture, Jul 66.
     (C) Msg, COMUSMACV to CINCPAC, 09365/25062 Mar 66.

144.   Ibid.

145. (S) Rpt, Hq USMACV, MACJ-5, Analysis of MACV Psywar Posture, Jul 66.
     (TS) Msg, JCS 4498, 5 Oct 66.

146. (C) MONEVAL, MACJ-341, Dec 66.

147. (C) Interview CHECO Personnel with Lt Col John McKechnie, MAC-PD, Dir/PsyOps, 22 May 1967.

148. (S) MONEVAL, MACJ-341, Jun 66.

149. (C) Rpt, History, 3d ARRGP, 1 Oct-31 Dec 66.

150.   Ibid.

151. (C) Rpt, History, 3d ARRGP, 1 Jul-30 Sep 66.
     (U) Briefing, 3d ARRGP by Capt. Jerry L. Larson, undated.

152. (TS) Trip Report Dr. John S. Foster, Jr., Dir/Defense Research and Engineering, 7 Jun 66.

153.   Ibid.

154. (C) Rpt, History, 3d ARRGP, 1 Oct-31 Dec 66.

155. (U) Briefing, 3dARRGP, by Capt Jerry L. Larson, undated.

156. (S) Special Report, CHECO, "USAF Search and Rescue in SEA, 1961-1966," 24 Oct 67.

157. (C) Rpt, History, 3d ARRGP, 1 Jul-30 Sep 66.

158.   Ibid.

159. (U) Monthly SAR Activity Report, Dec 66.

160. (TS) Msg, CINCPACAF to 7AF, 280203Z Sep 66.

FOOTNOTES

CHAPTER VI

1. (TS) Msg, COMUSMACV to CINCPAC, 081630Z, Jul 66.

2. (TS) Msg, COMUSMACV to CINCPAC, 081630Z, Jul 66.

3. (TS) Msg, COMUSMACV to CINCPAC, 070005Z, Aug 66.

4. (TS) MACVJ-2 Briefing for SECDEF, 10 Oct 66.

5. (TS) Msg, CINCPAC to JCS 26 Oct 66.

6. (S) Msg, COMUSMACV to CINCPAC, 021238Z Jan 67, subj: Year End Assessment of Enemy Situation and Strategy.

7. (S) MONEVAL Dec 66, MACJ 341.

8. Ibid.

9. (S) Msg, COMUSMACV to CINCPAC 021238Z Jan 67, subj: Year End Assessment of Enemy Situation & Strategy.

10. (S) MONEVAL Dec 66, MACJ-341.

11. (S) MACV Briefing for SECDEF 10 Oct 66.

12. Ibid.

13. Ibid.

14. (TS) Msg, from CINCPAC to JCS subj: Air Campaign Against North Vietnam, 26 Oct 66.

15. Ibid.

16. Ibid.

17. Ibid.

18. Ibid.

19. Ibid.

20. (TS) End of Tour Report - Maj Gen Gilbert L. Meyers, Deputy Commander of 2AD and 7AF, 23 Apr 65-1 Aug 66.

202

21. (C) Memo, RM 5214-ISA, Bombing North Vietnam: An Appraisal of Economic and Political Effects: Rand Corp, Dec 66.

22. Ibid.

23. (TS) Summary of SEA Air Operations (Jan-Nov 66) BG Joseph J. Kruzel, 13 Dec 66.

24. (S) Annual Supplement to Summary of Air Operations, SEA Calendar Year 1966, Hq PACAF; Mission Summary Data and Ordnance Data Sheets, Hq PACAF; 7AF (DOA) Staff Action Items, ltr dtd 12 Jan 67.

25. (S) Annual Supplement to Summary Air Operations in Southeast Asia Area, Calendar Year 1966, Hq PACAF; DOA 7AF Memo: Staff Action Items (Ltr, 7AF on 3 Jan 67), dtd 12 Jan 67.

26. (S) DOA 7AF memo: Staff Action Items (Ltr, 7AF, on 3 Jan 67) dtd 12 Jan 67.

27. (S) Annual Supplement to Summary Air Operations Southeast Asia Area, Calendar Year 1966, Hq PACAF.

28. (S) Command Status, Dec 66, Hq 7AF; Annual Supplement to Summary Air Operations Southeast Asia Area, Calendar Year 1966, Hq PACAF; DOA 7AF memo: Staff Action Items (Ltr, 7AF, 3 Jan 67) dtd 12 Jan 67.

29. (S) DOA 7AF memo: Staff Action Items (Ltr, 7AF, 3 Jan 67), dtd 12 Jan 67.

30. Ibid.

31. (S) MONEVAL DEC 1966, MACJ 341.

32. (S) Special Rpt No. 508, subj: Viet Cont/North Vietnamese Strategy in the Republic of Vietnam dtd 15 January 1967, Hq USARPAC.

33. Ibid.

34. Ibid.

35. Ibid.

36. Ibid.

37. Ibid.

38. Ibid.

39. Ibid.

APPENDIX I
ATTACKS ON AIR BASES-1966

Date	Airfield	Remarks
25 Jan	Da Nang	1 killed*, 6 wounded; little material and no aircraft damage.
20 Feb	An Khe	7 killed; 51 wounded; 8 helicopters damaged.
20 Feb	Binh Thuy	No U.S. casualties; 1 aircraft and some material damage.
7 Jul	Binh Thuy	1 killed; 4 wounded; 2 aircraft damaged; 1 destroyed.
13 Apr	Tan Son Nhut	**7 killed; 135 wounded; 56 aircraft damaged; 4 destroyed.
4 Dec	Tan Son Nhut	3 killed; 29 wounded; 18 aircraft damaged.
20 Apr	An Khe	2 aircraft damaged.
22 Apr	New Pleiku	Light damage and casualties.
18 May	Soc Trang Airfield	1 aircraft destroyed and 9 damaged.
22 Jun	Soc Trang Air Base	3 wounded; 19 aircraft damaged; 1 destroyed.
22 Jul	Quang Ngai	5 killed and 1 wounded.
23 Jul	Marble Mt. Air Facility, Da Nang	10 wounded and 23 aircraft damaged.
28 Aug	Vinh Long	7 aircraft damaged.
3 Sep	Camp Radcliff	4 killed; 61 wounded; 77 aircraft damaged or destroyed.
21 Sep	Chu Lai	16 wounded; 8 aircraft damaged.
22 Sep	Hammond Airfield	1 killed; 25 wounded; 15 aircraft damaged.
18 Oct	173d Abn Bde Base (Bien Hoa)	2 killed; 12 wounded; 1 aircraft destroyed.

* Only U.S. casualties are listed.
** See Project CHECO Study, "Mortar Attack Against Tan Son Nhut (Apr 66)."

GLOSSARY

AAA/AW	Antiaircraft Artillery/Automatic Weapons
ABCCC	Airborne Command and Control Center
ACC	Airlift Control Center
ACE	Airlift Control Elements
ACofS	Air Chief of Staff
ACS	Air Commando Squadron
ADLM	Air Delivered Land Mine
ADLMS	Air Delivered Land Mine System
AFAG	Air Force Advisory Group
AMC	Airborne Mission Commander
AO	Area of Operation
APC	Armored Personnel Carrier
ARVN	Army of the Republic of Vietnam
ARDF	Airborne Radio Direction Finding
ARRG	Aerospace Rescue and Recovery Group
ARRS	Aerospace Rescue and Recovery Squadron
ARVN	Army of the Republic of Vietnam
BDA	Bomb Damage Assessment
BR	BARREL ROLL
CAP	Combat Air Patrol (SARCAP, MIGCAP, RESCAP)
CAS	Close Air Support
CBU	Cluster Bomb Unit
CES	Civil Engineering Squadron
CHICOM	Chinese Communist
CINCPAC	Commander in Chief, Pacific
CINCPACAF	Commander in Chief, Pacific Air Forces
CINCPACFLT	Commander in Chief, Pacific Fleet
CJCS	Chairman, Joint Chiefs of Staff
COC	Combat Operations Center
Combat Saves	Saves made as result of enemy actions or in retrieving personnel from hostile area
COMINT	Communications Intelligence
COMUSMACV	Commander, U.S. Military Assistance Command, Vietnam
CONUS	Continental United States
COSVN	Central Office South Vietnam
CRC	Combat Reporting Center
CRP	Control Reporting Point
CSAF	Chief of Staff, Air Force
CSG	Combat Support Group
CTF	Corps Task Force
CTZ	Corps Tactical Zone
CVA	Assault Aircraft Carrier (USN)
CY	Calendar Year

DAS	Direct Air Support Center
DME	Distance Measuring Equipment
DMZ	Demilitarized Zone
DRV	Democratic Republic of Vietnam (North Vietnam)
EARS	Emergency Airlift Request Systems
ECM	Electronic Countermeasure(s)
ELINT	Electronics Intelligence
EW/GCI	Early Warning, Ground Controlled Intercept
FAC	Forward Air Controller
FAR	Force Armee Royale
FIS	Fighter Interceptor Squadron
FSB	Fire Support Base
FWF	Free World Forces
FWMAF	Free World Military Assistance Forces
GCI	Ground Controlled Intercept
GVN	Government, Republic of Vietnam
HE	High Explosives
HF	High Frequency
ICC	International Control Commission
IRAN	Inspect, Repair as Necessary
JAGO	Joint/Air Ground Operation
JCS	Joint Chiefs of Staff
JGS	Joint General Staff
JOC	Joint Operations Center
JPRC	Joint Personnel Recovery Center
JSARC	Joint Search and Rescue Center
KBA	Killed by Air
KIA	Killed in Action
LIMDIS	Limited Distribution
LOC	Line of Communication
MAF	Marine Amphibious Force
MAW	Marine Air Wing
MCP	Military Construction Program
MOB	Main Operating Base
NAVAIR	Naval Air Operations
NAVLO	Navy Liaison Officer
NFLSVN	National Front for the Liberation of South Vietnam
NLF	National Liberation Front
NMCC	National Military Command Center

NM	Nautical Miles
Non-Combat Saves	Saves not made as direct result of hostile action or environment
NORM	Not Operational Ready, Maintenance
NORS	Not Operational Ready, Supply
NVA	North Vietnamese Army
NVN	North Vietnam
OICC	Officer in Charge of Construction
OPLAN	Operations Plan
OPORD	Operations Order
PACAF	Pacific Air Forces
PAR	Peacetime Aerial Reconnaissance
PAVN	Peoples Army of Vietnam
PCC	Personnel Control Center
POL	Petroleum, Oil and Lubricants
Psyops	Psychological Operations
Psywar	Psychological Warfare
RAAF	Royal Australian Air Force
RESCORT	Role of Escort
RLAF	Royal Laotian Air Force
RLG	Royal Laotian Government
RTG	Royal Thai Government
RVN	Republic of Vietnam
RVNAF	South Vietnamese Air Force
SACLO	Strategic Air Command Liaison Officer
SAM	Surface-to-Air Missile
SAR	Search and Rescue
SEA	Southeast Asia
SECDEF	Secretary of Defense
SL	STEEL TIGER
SVN	South Vietnam
TAC	Tactical Air Command
TACAN	Tactical Air Control and Navigation
TACC	Tactical Air Control Center
TACC-NS	Tactical Air Control Center--North Sector
TACS	Tactical Air Control System
TCS	Tactical Composite Squadron
TFS	Tactical Fighter Squadron
TFW	Tactical Fighter Wing
TOC	Tactical Operations Center
TRS	Tactical Reconnaissance Center
TTY	Teletypewriter
TUOC	Tactical Unit Operations Center

UCMJ	Universal Code of Military Justice
UE	Unit Equipment
USAIRA	U.S. Air Attache
USMACTHAI	United States Military Assistance Command, Thailand
USMACV	United States Military Assistance Command, Vietnam
UHF	Ultra High Frequency
USSR	Union of Soviet Socialist Republics
VC	Viet Cong
VHF	Very High Frequency
VNAF	South Vietnamese Air Force
WAAPM	Wide Area Antipersonnel Mine
WAIS	Weekly Air Intelligence Summary
WBA	Wounded by Air
WIA	Wounded in Action
WRM	War Readiness Material